LITERATURE
THROUGH THE EYES OF FAITH

LITERATURE THROUGH THE EYES OF FAITH

Susan V. Gallagher
and
Roger Lundin

Christian College Coalition
For Enduring Values

HarperSanFrancisco
A Division of HarperCollinsPublishers

Library of Congress Cataloging-in-Publication Data
Lundin, Roger.
   Literature through the eyes of faith.
    1. Christianity and literature.   2. Christianity
in literature.   I. Gallagher, Susan V.   II. Title.
PN49.L86   1989   809   88-45684
ISBN 0-06-065318-3 (pbk.)

94 95 96 MAL 10 9 8 7 6 5

CONTENTS

FOREWORD

There have always been theoretical issues concerning the composition and reading of literature and concerning the nature of the literary text. And there have always been *controversies* concerning the answers to these issues. Until quite recently, however, most teachers of literature apparently felt that such issues could be avoided—many felt that they *should* be avoided. Literature, they felt, could be read and appreciated without entering the controversies of theorists.

That day of innocence is rapidly disappearing. To more and more teachers of literature it is becoming evident that the way they had been reading and appreciating literature did not steer clear of the issues raised by theorists but took positions on those issues. So too, what they had been saying about the literary text took stands on such issues. And the texts they had their students read did not reflect some purely objective recognition of greatness but presupposed certain values with which other intelligent and committed people disagreed.

Literature, which once appeared to be a resting place from the rigors of theory, has become a battleground of theory.

One of the great merits of this new book by professors Gallagher and Lundin is that, in their approach to literature, they openly and straightforwardly enter this battleground. They do not try to go around it. With courageous honesty they face up to the issues, lay them out clearly, and frequently themselves take a stand. They do so in graceful, readable prose. And more remarkably, perhaps, they do not forget literature in the excitement of engaging in the theoretical debates. They never forget that the point is not to keep theorists busy but to illuminate literature.

This would be enough to make this book a significant contribution. But I have not yet mentioned its chief distinction. Professors Gallagher and Lundin have not simply added another book to the ongoing discussion about literature. Their guiding question is this: *How does literature look when seen through the eyes of faith*—by someone informed on the theoretical issues? The shape of their book has been determined by their address to those questions which, in their judgment, a reflective Christian should be raising when engaged with literature.

In the course of addressing themselves to these questions, Gallagher and Lundin begin to work out a fresh and imaginative approach to literature. Most Christian reflections on literature, over the last century, have been, in a rough-and-ready way, Romantic. Gallagher and Lundin believe that a Romantic approach can no longer be defended. This is one of the very first attempts to provide a Christian perspective on literature which is non-Romantic in character. It is not an exaggeration to say that their work is path-breaking.

This book thus achieves that almost impossible task of being of interest both to the Christian who just wants some basic questions about literature discussed, and to the Christian who has read around in the recent theoretical disputes about literature and wants some illumination on those confusing disputes. At the same time it will be of interest to the non-Christian who wants to see how two gifted scholars who care very much about literature, who are deeply committed to the Christian faith, and who are eminently informed about the recent disputes in critical theory, struggle to bring together into a creative whole these sides of their existence. In our fragmented world, such attempts at wholeness are uncommon. When we come across them, we can all learn.

Nicholas Wolterstorff
Professor of Philosophy
Calvin College &
The Free University of Amsterdam

PREFACE

This book explores the relationship of the Christian faith to the study of literature. Its goal is to help students of literature understand more clearly the nature of language and literature, to acquaint them with the tools of literary study, and to introduce them to the rich history of Christian reflection on literature, language, and the reading experience. To that end, we have included in the book discussions of the theory and history of literature as well as practical advice for the study of it. We have sought to make our general points about literature by exploring specific examples of literary art.

Though this book represents a joint effort, each of us has had specific responsibility for separate chapters. There are some, though not many, first-person references in the individual chapters. Rather than remove them, and in order to avoid any confusion, we have thought it best to indicate which one of us wrote each chapter. The Introduction was written by both of us. Roger Lundin wrote chapters 1, 2, 3, 6, 7, and 8; Susan Gallagher wrote chapters 4, 5, 9, 10, 11, 12, and 13.

We are especially grateful to Nicholas Wolterstorff for his leadership and encouragement. We thank the members of our task force—Gaymon Bennett, Edward Ericson, Paul Nisly, Ann Paton, and Nancy Tischler—for the scrutiny they have given to our work and the support they have given to us in this project. In addition, we are grateful for the many insightful comments we received from English professors from the member colleges of the Christian College Coalition. And finally, we thank Karen Longman of the Christian College Coalition for her patience, steadiness, and encouragement throughout the long course of this project.

INTRODUCTION: LITERATURE AND THE CHRISTIAN

The two of us have written this book out of our conviction that reading literature can be a vital and enjoyable activity. We will argue that the writing and reading of literature are forms of human action and, as such, have the same potential for good or evil as any of our actions. Great literature, art, and music cannot guarantee that those who appreciate them will be capable of great actions, or even decent ones. The authorities who supervised the ovens of the Nazi concentration camps during the day passed the time at night by reading Goethe's *Faust* or enjoying the symphonies of Beethoven and Brahms. In this book, we will encourage you to discover the value and delights of literature, but we will not claim that literature embodies beauty and goodness in a way unique unto itself. Like all human actions, works of literature are a part of history, and history is as much a story of tragedy and terror as it is a tale of truth and beauty.

Furthermore, as a subject of study, literature itself has a history, for ideas about it have changed dramatically over the centuries. Because the answers given to the questions "What is literature?" and "Why should I read it?" have varied considerably over time, the person trying to define "literature" ought to understand something of the history of modern ideas about it. It is especially important to do so in this book, for in discussing the writing and reading of literature as forms of human action, the two of us will be taking issue with several crucial assumptions behind modern definitions of literature.

Literature on the Defensive

Because in recent history literature has often found itself in opposition to science, to understand modern views about literature, we must recognize the dominance of science in our culture. For several centuries, the sciences have set the standards of truth for Western culture, and their undeniable usefulness in helping us to organize, analyze, and manipulate facts has given them an unprecedented importance in modern societies.

Many of the significant developments in modern science began in the seventeenth and eighteenth centuries. For example, the work of the great English scientist and mathematician, Sir Isaac Newton, was particularly important in shaping the modern understanding of the world. With the law of gravity, Newton discovered the universal force governing the motion of objects and thus demonstrated that the world was an amazingly complex mechanism operating according to well-established laws. The technological advancements of the Industrial Revolution, which soon followed Newton's discoveries, seemed to confirm the usefulness of thinking of the world as a great mechanism.

As the image of the world as machine took hold of the Western imagination, a number of people began to wonder what could be the role of the arts in such a world. For example, what good could poetry do, once it had been discovered that all things operated according to the laws of mechanics? Poetry might provide harmless amusement for those who needed such diversions, but to claim anything more for it would be foolish. When Newton himself was asked for his judgment of poetry, he replied: "I'll tell you that of [Isaac] Barrow [an English mathematician and theologian]:—he said, that poetry was a kind of ingenious nonsense" (Abrams, *Mirror*, 300). Similarly, Thomas Sprat, an English historian of science during Newton's time, wrote of the danger of poetic images. "Poets of old devis'd a thousand false" visions, Sprat explained:

But, from the time in which the *Real Philosophy* has appear'd, there is scarce any whisper remaining of such *horrors*. . . . The course of things goes quietly along, in its own true channel of *Natural Causes and Effects*. For this we are beholden to *Experiments;* which though they have not yet completed the Discovery of the true world, yet they have already vanquish'd those wild inhabitants of the false world, that us'd to astonish the minds of Men. (Abrams, *Mirror*, 266)

In this passage, Sprat argues that stories and poetic images (the "horrors" and "wild inhabitants" to which he refers) are harmful because they give us an untrue picture of the world. Sprat is relieved that the scientific discoveries of his day (the "Real Philosophy" of Newton and others) have rid the world of the superstitions "that us'd to astonish the minds of Men."

But there were many, especially the Romantic poets and essayists of the early nineteenth century, who viewed with alarm the banishing of these "wild inhabitants" from the world. For example, the English Romantic poet John Keats believed that the Newtonian view of reality threatened to destroy our ability to see the beauty of the world. Keats feared that a world in which myths and poetic visions had vanished would become a barren and uninviting place. In *Lamia,* he wrote of the destructive, disenchanting power of science (which he calls "philosophy" here):

> Do not all charms fly
> At the mere touch of cold philosophy?
> There was an awful rainbow once in heaven:
> We know her woof, her texture; she is given
> In the dull catalogue of common things.
> Philosophy will clip an Angel's wings,
> Conquer all mysteries by rule and line,
> Empty the haunted air, and gnomed mine—
> Unweave a rainbow.

Note the verbs that Keats uses to describe the power of science. It "clips," "conquers," "empties," and "unweaves" the mysteries of the world, leaving us with a dull vision of reality. For centuries the rainbow had stood as a symbol of God's terrifying power and reassuring promise, but once it had been exhaustively described by science, the beautiful bow in the sky became just one more phenomenon explained by the laws of vision. In a world in which mechanical laws could explain everything, Keats wondered, how might a person remain reverent in the presence of the wonders of creation?

It is revealing to compare Keats's lament with an earlier vision of the relationship of poetry to the created order. In the late middle ages, Dante wrote the *Divine Comedy*. In the poem, as he makes his way through hell, purgatory, and heaven, Dante finds himself unable to describe the horrors and splendors he sees in God's created realms. At the very end of the *Divine Comedy*, he tries to describe his vision of the powerful beauty behind all creation. He struggles to find the appropriate words to depict the wonder he has beheld:

> For the great imagination here power failed;
> but already my desire and will [in harmony]
> were turning like a wheel moved evenly
> by the Love which turns the sun and the other stars.

At the close of the *Divine Comedy*, then, the heavenly world appears too stunning and beautiful to be depicted adequately by the poet. God and his creation are more majestic than any images the poet can create and more astonishing than anything he can imagine. In Dante's world, if the poet is to be faulted, it is because his vision falls short of the splendor it tries to depict.

But in the modern scientific world of Newton and Sprat, the poet has a different liability. Rather than a valiant struggle to describe the indescribable, the poet's work may appear to be a trivial nuisance which diverts us from the hard facts of life. According to this view, poetry is not inadequate. It is simply irrelevant.

In response to this "scientific" view of the usefulness of poetry, poets such as Keats made new and grand claims for their art. Yes, they agreed, science is right to say that the rainbow might not possess in itself the wonderful qualities we have long found in it. As a physical phenomenon, it may be only one more fact to be catalogued by the laws of science. The only way to see it as a sign of spiritual power and comfort is for the imaginative person to weave beautiful images around it. If the rainbow is to appear as a symbol of spiritual truth and comfort, then the poet must create the beautiful garment to adorn it.

Many poets of the Romantic age and later periods believed they had discovered the key to literature in this power to adorn the world with beauty. Though poetry might not be able to change reality, it could conjure up enchanting alternatives to our ordinary experiences. At the beginning of *Endymion*, Keats celebrates the consoling power of "things of beauty":

> A thing of beauty is a joy forever:
> Its loveliness increases; it will never
> Pass into nothingness; but still will keep
> A bower quiet for us, and a sleep
> Full of sweet dreams, and health, and quiet breathing.

The poet Samuel Taylor Coleridge, a contemporary of Keats, also lamented the loss of wonder in modern life. In "Dejection: An Ode," Coleridge depicts the human spirit as a dispirited bystander who looks without feeling upon a natural world unrelated to him:

> All this long eve, so balmy and serene,
> Have I been gazing on the western sky,
> And its peculiar tint of yellow green:
> And still I gaze—and with how blank an eye!
> . . . Though I should gaze forever
> On that green light that lingers in the west:
> I may not hope from outward forms to win
> The passion and the life, whose fountains are within.

If we are to find anything beautiful or passionate in the world, Coleridge argues, it must come from the "fountains within," for while the spirit of the poet is lively, the world of nature seems lifeless and unresponsive. According to the poem, the consolation available to us is that of seeing how the imagination can bring the dead world back to life:

> O Lady! we receive but what we give,
> And in our life alone does Nature live . . .
>   Ah! from the soul itself must issue forth
> A light, a glory, a fair luminous cloud
>   Enveloping the Earth—

The poems by Keats and Coleridge, then, praise the power of human creativity. In doing so, the poets rightly celebrate the human ability to give order to experience in fresh and satisfying ways. At the same time, however, there is also something troubling in the Romantic glorification of our creative powers. In responding to the lifelessness of the mechanistic view of the world, the Romantic poets all but deified the imagination. Because they valued human creativity as a source of lively power in a dreary world, they were willing to ascribe to the imagination powers that for centuries had been attributed to God alone.

In the nineteenth century, the celebration of the life-giving power of poetry became a commonplace of thinking about the arts. The American poet Emily Dickinson, for example, often developed themes of this kind in her poems. In "I reckon—when I count at all—," Dickinson lists the things that matter most in life. To her surprise, she discovers that one item on the list seems to sum up them all:

> I reckon—when I count at all—
> First—Poets—Then the Sun—
> Then Summer—Then the Heaven of God—
> And then—the List is done—
>
> But, looking back—the First so seems
> To Comprehend the Whole—
> The Others look a needless Show—
> So I write—Poets—All—

Their Summer—lasts a Solid Year—
They can afford a Sun
The East—would deem extravagant—
And if the Further Heaven—

Be Beautiful as they prepare
For Those who worship Them—
It is too difficult a Grace—
To justify the Dream—

Why do the Summer, the Sun, and the Heaven of God seem insignificant when compared to the Poet? It is because God's summer "falls" away each year, while the Poet can create a Summer which "lasts a Solid Year." Furthermore, the Sun created by the Poet is more grand than the one that rises each morning in the east. And, finally, the promised Heaven of Christian faith is too far from us and too difficult for us to attain; it cannot compare favorably with the heavenly visions offered to us *now* by the Poet.

The justifications that Keats, Coleridge, and Dickinson offer for poetry are typical of the defense presented on behalf of literature in the western world for the last two hundred years. In Romantic theories about literature, it is commonly claimed that since science and technology have alienated us from nature and one another, only the imagination can make us whole again. The poet can create images to heal our wounds and console our hearts. As readers, we turn to literature for the comfort, diversion, and enlightenment that are denied to us in our everyday life. The *real* world may be lost beyond hope, but in the *imaginative* realm, the poet can find for us "A bower quiet . . . and a sleep/ Full of sweet dreams, and health, and quiet breathing."

Dante or a Soap Opera?

How does the Christian student justify spending time studying poems and plays if they are primarily diversions from the real world? All of us need rest and refreshment, but if literature and the arts are primarily means to those ends, why not indulge in more enjoyable ways of reaching the same goals? Why should we read Dante or Dickinson, that is, when we can have a better time watching a soap opera, a game show, or a music video?

In responding to questions such as these, which are really questions about how literature can claim to be a unique and important activity if its primary purpose is to give us pleasure, the defenders of literature have often stressed that although other activities give us enjoyment and comfort, only the arts can offer us pleasures unblemished by selfishness. Our normal pleasures play upon our greed, lust, or hunger for power, they argue, but the appreciation of a work of art offers us a chance to satisfy our desires without harming others. Such appreciation of beauty is supposedly *disinterested*. According to this view of literature, when we gaze at a landscape painting, we can "own the land" without depriving others of it; and when we read a novel about human conflict, we can experience the tension vicariously without harming ourselves or others.

In a letter written in 1817, Keats made an argument of this kind in support of literature when he praised what he called "*Negative Capability*, that is when man is capable of being in uncertainties, Mysteries, doubts, without any irritable reaching after fact & reason." In other words, in an experience of art we set aside our typical cares and our passion for certainty. By contemplating beauty in all its complexity, we broaden our minds and make our imaginations lively. According to this line of argument, once we have read a great piece of literature, we can return to our everyday experiences refreshed for the tasks before us.

The poet Robert Frost describes such an experience in "Birches." The boy in this poem likes to climb and balance carefully on the branches of birch trees, returning to the ground only when his weight has begun to bend the branch back to the earth. For Frost, the boy who swings on birches is like the man who writes poems; both of them do these things to get away from their painful cares:

> So was I once myself a swinger of birches.
> And so I dream of going back to be.

It's when I'm weary of considerations,
And life is too much like a pathless wood
Where your face burns and tickles with the cobwebs
Broken across it, and one eye is weeping
From a twig's having lashed across it open.
I'd like to get away from earth awhile
And then come back to it and begin over.
May no fate willfully misunderstand me
And half grant what I wish and snatch me away
Not to return. Earth's the right place for love:
I don't know where it's likely to go better.

It is in those moments, the poem says, when life seems too much like a pathless wood in which you are stung and lashed by difficulties, that you climb out of pain for a while and into the pleasures of poetry.

The contemporary critic Northrop Frye makes a similar point when he claims that literature can transform our everyday experience. Frye, whose work has had an enormous influence on Christian thinking about literature, draws a sharp distinction between our "environment" and "home." Our "environment" is the world we are cast into as biological and social creatures. It is the world of the biological, political, and economic forces that shape our lives. This is an "alien" world in which the desires of our heart have no influence on the laws that rule our lives. Frye claims that in the works of the imagination, however, we are ushered into an ideal "home" created by the human mind. In this world, "anything goes," because any dream can be realized, any vision fulfilled. In the realm of the imagination there are no limits to human ability, and the poet's "job is not to describe nature, but to show you a world completely absorbed and possessed by the human mind." Instead of describing life's painful realities, the poet helps people to catch a glimpse of unspeakable beauty. "Literature does not reflect life, but it doesn't escape or withdraw from life either: it swallows it. And the imagination won't stop until it's swallowed everything" (*Educated Imagination*, 32–33, 80).

According to this view, poetry and fiction have the power to lead us to satisfaction and safety. They carry us out of the real world

"Where your face burns and tickles with the cobwebs/Broken across it, and one eye is weeping/From a twig's having lashed across it open." We journey from that world to the realm of literature, where we take comfort in the delights offered to our minds and senses. In the world built by human creativity, the troubling realities of ordinary life are transformed by our redemptive imagination.

Creation and Incarnation

As attractive as this view of literature has been to many Christians, some elements of it conflict with Christian belief, while other parts of it are at odds with recent discoveries about the nature of language. The Christian student of literature ought to ground his or her thinking in the Scriptures and in the central doctrines of the Christian tradition. In addition, Christian thinking about literature needs to consider the dramatic developments of recent decades in the study of language, science, and the arts, because much has changed since the Romantic poets formulated their grand defenses of literature.

There is a limited truth to the view of literature as a form of escape providing a pleasing alternative to life as we commonly experience it. We do need occasional diversion from the cares and terrors of life, and at times we may seek, in reading, an escape from our predicaments. But there is also for the Christian something troubling about a view that focuses upon the unsatisfying nature of the world and upon our need to escape from it. Indeed, the doctrines of Creation and Incarnation challenge any claim that the world is inherently evil or irredeemably flawed. When God created the heavens and earth, he said they were *good*, rather than evil or alien. Of course, sin has made the world a far more difficult place than God intended it to be in its perfection. But few Christians would argue that sin has completely destroyed the goodness that God poured into creation and continues to impart to his world.

As Christians, we can begin thinking about literature by acknowledging that the world has beauty and an underlying order to which God has called us to respond. Theories that sharply contrast the satisfactions of literature with the dissatisfactions of life fail to acknowledge the goodness of God's creation and run the risk of deifying the human imagination. By ascribing to the human spirit all but unlimited powers, these theories about literature are in danger of violating the First Commandment: "Thou shalt have no other Gods before me." As we praise human creativity, we need to remind ourselves that no matter how imaginative we are, we remain God's creatures and that all of us have "sinned and fall short of the glory of God." Though there may be certain similarities between our abilities to create works of literature and God's power to create the world, our sin and creatureliness dramatically limit our powers. None of us is God.

In addition to the doctrine of Creation, the Incarnation also plays an important role in Christian thinking about literature. In recent decades, Christian poets and essayists have frequently written about the *incarnational* power of literature, by which they mean its ability to embody truth in a unique manner. It is often said that the poet *incarnates* meaning by revealing profound and timeless truths through the use of concrete images and stories. In a poem, spirit (abstract thoughts) and flesh (concrete images) are supposed to become one, just as God revealed himself in the human form of Jesus of Nazareth.

Although this is an appealing view of the poet's powers and calling, it may not be appropriate to consider the Incarnation as a timeless principle embodied in the exercise of the human imagination. For, rather than being an abstract principle or category of thought, the Incarnation is most importantly an event that took place *once* in time. According to the doctrine of the Incarnation, the miraculous fact is that the Word became flesh and dwelt among us. The scandal of the Christian faith is that God walked the earth as a carpenter in first-century Palestine and died on a cross on our behalf. The Apostle Paul challenges the Philippians:

Your attitude should be the same as that of Christ Jesus: Who being in very nature God, did not consider equality with God something to be grasped, but made himself nothing, taking the very nature of a servant, being made in human likeness. And being found in appearance as a man, he humbled himself and became obedient to death—even death on a cross! (Philippians 2:5–8)

Many of us have no doubt considered what Paul's charge to the Philippians means for our relationships with one another. But it also has implications for the way we think about literature. The passage speaks of a God who, instead of scorning the world his creatures had damaged, chose to live in it and die for it. The action of God in Christ calls into question Christian attitudes that find the world so displeasing that they celebrate literature because it helps us flee to imagined realms. A Christian reader can relish the refreshment and relaxation offered by literature without finding the imagination superior to the world God has created and for which his son suffered and died.

In short, in this book we will promote the study of literature by emphasizing that God in Creation made all things good and that in the Incarnation he gave us his Son to make right what we have made wrong. Though literature can provide us with relaxation and with images of the world as it might ideally be, it is neither an escape from reality nor a saving transformation of it. Instead, it enables us to respond to the order, beauty, and grace of God and his world and to the disorder that our sin has brought into that world.

What is Literature?

In literature, people try out ideas. What if this happened? What if someone felt this way? Would this view of life give meaning to my life? Are these words beautiful when they are put together in this way? Are these events entertaining? Reading brings us into the real world. The words that compose literary texts do not belong solely to an imaginary realm. Instead, they have meanings and consequences, even as the words that we say to our parents and friends do. When we read, we participate in life as we see how books structure, interpret, and communicate experiences and truths.

Consider the love poetry of William Shakespeare. The scientist might ask, "Why read a poem about romantic agony when we can do psychological research that reveals how we can overcome our anxieties?" The Romantic poet might reply, "Because the love imaginatively embodied in poetry is an ideal, glorious love far surpassing your boring data about relationships."

But literature both comes out of and affects the world that God created, or what Frye would call our "environment." When Shakespeare wrote his poems, he drew on Renaissance ideas about love even as he crafted the poetic lines and chose particular words to create a certain effect. As we read his poems, we interpret their ideas in the light of our own experiences, and in so doing, we relate them to our own world of romantic attachments and feelings. When we read Shakespeare's love poetry, we live in and interact with God's created world.

Speaking about works of art in general, the Christian philosopher Nicholas Wolterstorff suggests that they are not only objects of enjoyment and contemplation but also "instruments and objects of action" (15–16). Similarly, literary texts are not merely imaginative creations, but also instruments composed of language that we use to perform certain activities, such as thinking about social issues, moral questions, or personal feelings.

A piece of writing is a tool for action. Think, for example, of the written instructions accompanying your new VCR. Reading such a text makes it possible (you hope) for you to perform the action of loading and playing a movie or taping your favorite television show. The ideas communicated through the text make a practical difference in your life. In a similar way, poems and stories can bring things to your attention in such a way that you might begin to think differently about something and then go on to act on these new thoughts in a very concrete way. Reading texts enables us to participate in life, not to escape it.

The Many Sides of Literature

When thinking about how literature provides a way for us to interact with our world, we should realize that literature makes possible many different actions. Books can serve a variety of purposes. They can be used for practical ends (instructions for running your VCR), social ends (a love letter), liturgical ends (the Apostles' Creed), and aesthetic ends (a Japanese haiku). Texts can provide enjoyment, represent a world, voice the conscious statements of the author, express more than the author planned, or allow us to appreciate the author's skill and the beauty of certain combinations of words.

However, not all literature is useful for all purposes. We can use many works of literature for multiple purposes; others may serve only one. Some texts teach, others amuse, others give us joy in the gifts of God. All provide various ways to participate in God's world.

To understand a text, we must see its context. Authors form literary works by employing particular conventions, such as presenting words in poetic lines or placing characters into certain situations. Readers respond by using appropriate interpretive skills, by reading differently the different kinds of texts that they encounter. Few people now read Edward Gibbon's *The History of the Decline and Fall of the Roman Empire* for its factual information or statistics; instead, readers now look at its rhetorical strategies, cultural attitudes, and interpretive methods. Similarly, an Afro-American folk-tune that was sung while picking cotton, or a personal journal entry, can perform other functions when presented in the context of a literary anthology. Even the Bible can be read in various ways: readers may try to understand a particular theological doctrine, attempt to find personal guidance, or admire and enjoy the beauty of its poetic expressions of praise.

As contexts change, so may functions: in a church service, a hymn is an instrument of praise; in a poetry class, it may become an instrument of aesthetic delight as well as an instrument revealing the Catholic theology of its author. In 1776, the American Declaration of Independence was an act of political rebellion; today when we read it in history class, it is a document of social (and educational) significance; when we read it as American literature, it demonstrates in its structure and content the rationalism and deism of America's founding fathers.

The rest of this book will look in more detail at the issues raised by the view that we participate in the world by reading literature. We will examine why, given the nature of literature and our Christian responsibilities, we should read. We will explore the reading process itself to find out what kinds of actions take place as we read. And we will consider how Christians can make wise choices about what they read and how they evaluate it.

PART 1

Why Should We Read Literature?

Chapter 1

UNDERSTANDING OUR
EXPERIENCE

A Christian understanding of literature is grounded in beliefs derived from the Scriptures and developed through the course of Christian history. These beliefs provide the foundation for our attempts to explain the nature of literature and what it is that we do when we read it. For centuries in the Western world, Christian reflection upon interpretation—especially the "reading" of the Scriptures and of nature—deeply informed the practice and theory of interpretation for all written works. With the dramatic growth of secular thinking in the past several centuries, the influence of Christian thought upon literary study has become less explicit, even though the careful observer may still discover beneath the surface of contemporary thinking deep Christian roots.

Nevertheless, whether contemporary beliefs about literature show the historic influence of Christianity or its present insignificance, the task for the Christian student of literature remains that of grounding his or her thinking in the history of Christian thought. And one place for the Christian to begin thinking about literature is with the conviction, held by Christians through the ages, that in a universe created and ruled by a sovereign God all things are meaningful. The Scriptures proclaim that, in creating the world, God gave order and purpose to it, that in the Incarnation he sent his Son to redeem our fallen state, and that at the end of the age he will judge the nations and disclose the meaning of history in its fullness.

The loss of faith in a God who creates, reveals, and redeems is no doubt a major source of the sense of meaninglessness one finds in much modern literature. It is this loss of meaning, for example, that the American novelist Herman Melville contemplates in a passage from *Moby-Dick*. In the novel, Captain Ahab is driven by a passionate desire to discover the truth about life by slaying a whale called Moby Dick. As an incentive to his crew, Ahab nails a gold coin to one of his ship's posts. This reward will go to the first person to spot Moby Dick. Ishmael, the narrator of the novel, reports that one day Ahab pauses as he passes the coin:

> . . . he seemed to be newly attracted by the strange figures and inscriptions stamped on it, as though now for the first time beginning to interpret for himself in some monomaniac way whatever significance might lurk in them. And some certain significance lurks in all things, else all things are little worth, and the round world itself but an empty cipher, except to sell by the cartload, as they do hills about Boston, to fill up some morass in the Milky Way. (358)

In a Christian doctrine of Creation, the earth is much more than a cartload of dirt filling a hole in a corner of the Milky Way. In its abundance and complexity—as the Psalmist, the Apostle Paul, and many through the ages have proclaimed—the world gives evidence of having been the creation of God. God "has been pleased," wrote John Calvin in *Institutes of the Christian Religion*, "to manifest his perfections in the whole structure of the universe. . . . On each of his works his glory is engraven in characters so bright, so distinct, and so illustrious, that none, however dull and illiterate, can plead ignorance as their excuse" (1: 51).

The doctrine of the Incarnation also testifies to the significance of earthly life. Though we have all sinned, God has neither destroyed nor abandoned humanity. We are not alone in our sins, the Gospel assures us, and the events of our lives are not the products of a cruel fate or random process. "So the Word was made flesh, in order that sin, destroyed by means of that same flesh through which it had gained the mastery and taken hold and lorded it, should no longer be in us," explains the second-century theologian Irenaus, "and therefore our Lord took up the same first formation for an incarnation, that so he might join battle on behalf of his forefathers, and overcome through Adam what had stricken us through Adam" (Pelikan, 1: 144–145).

Thus, the doctrines of Creation and Incarnation affirm that human life is inherently meaningful. God has placed us in a world filled with order and hints of wonder, and through his acts of revelation and redemption he has entered into our history. As a result, although some things are obviously of greater importance than others, everything in our experience has significance, and our attempt to discern that significance—as well as we can—is part of our calling as God's servants.

If we are convinced that our world has meaning, then we may see that interpretation is not isolated from the rest of life but is at the very heart of our life. The English teacher who scours a poem for symbols is not an odd person obsessed with meaning, for every one of us is always "reading experience." The anxious student wants to know what her teacher means when he clasps his hands behind his head and stares off in the distance before answering her question; the job seeker tries to interpret the signals she receives from a potential employer during an interview; and the son tries to read between the lines of his parents' latest letter to him at college.

Symbols and Meaning

Many modern works of literature focus upon questions of meaning and understanding, as do a number of classics from the past. For example, though Shakespeare's *King Lear* was written almost four hundred years ago, it seems contemporary in its concern with interpretation and matters of meaning. The central character of the play, Lear, is an aging king who wants to finish his life in peace. To that end, he decides to divide his kingdom among his three daughters. In doing so, he hopes to avoid any conflict among his heirs after his death. Though he will relinquish authority, he plans to keep a group of knights as a symbol of his former power and to travel with this entourage from daughter to daughter in his final years.

Things go wrong for Lear, however. To decide how he should break up his kingdom, he devises a test of love for his daughters. He requires that each express her love to him, and two of them, Goneril and Regan, pass with high marks. But as they praise their father, their sister Cordelia concludes that she cannot match their hollow praise and resolves to say "nothing." "I love your Majesty / According to my bond, nor more nor less," she tells her father. Angered by her refusal to flatter him, the king banishes Cordelia from the kingdom and divides the land between Goneril and Regan.

Though Lear hopes to hold on to the symbols of kingship while giving up its responsibilities, Goneril and Regan have different plans. They see their father as an unstable old man who may go back on his word and attempt to reclaim the authority he has given them. Realizing that they face the possible loss of all they have acquired, Goneril and Regan set out to strip Lear of his remaining power and dignity. To that end, they determine to take from him his knights, the symbols he has kept as a reminder of his former authority.

Lear and those who still serve him are quick to notice the change in his status. His knight says that Lear is not treated with the same ceremony and civility as he had been; Goneril's servant calls Lear not "my Lord" but rather "my lady's father"; and Lear's Fool, a court jester of sorts, says that Lear is an empty egg-shell, a zero without a number before it, and a shelled pea-pod. When Lear cries out, "Who is it that can tell me who I am?" his Fool replies, "Lear's shadow."

At this point, a reader might ask, "What is the problem? After all, these are only metaphors and symbols. What does it matter that people no longer see Lear as a significant man?" The Fool could answer these questions, because he knows what is at stake in Lear's having given up power. That is why he chooses images with a quality of emptiness to describe his weakened king. These images depict form without content, for the Fool knows that Lear had been foolish to believe he could retain the symbols of power without bearing its burdens.

As Lear struggles to retain his dignity, his daughters taunt him about the number of knights he wishes to keep in his service:

LEAR   What, must I come to you
         With five–and–twenty? Regan, said you so?
REGAN   And speak't again, my lord. No more with me.
LEAR   . . . [*To Goneril*] I'll go with thee.
         Thy fifty yet doth double five-and-twenty,
         And thou art twice her love.
GONERIL Hear me, my lord.
         What need you five-and-twenty? ten? or five?
         To follow in a house where twice so many
         Have a command to tend you?
REGAN   What need one?
LEAR   O reason not the need! Our basest beggars
         Are in the poorest thing superfluous.
         Allow not nature more than nature needs,
         Man's life is cheap as beast's. Thou art a lady:
         If only to go warm were gorgeous,
         Why nature needs not what thou gorgeous wears't,
         Which scarcely keeps thee warm. But, for true need. . . .

                                        (2.4. 248–65)

Goneril and Regan argue that as a matter of practicality, Lear does not need to have any knights with him. The knights are rowdy, and the daughters can provide whatever service or protection their father needs. To their calculating claims, Lear can only cry out, "O reason not the need!" If life is only a matter of mechanics and calculation, he asks, why do his daughters dress themselves in such splendor? We have been created to make symbols and seek meaning, Lear argues, and everything in our life is significant. Everything *signifies* something. If the symbols with which we surround ourselves mean nothing, then our lives also mean little or nothing, because they have no *human* purpose: "Allow not nature more than nature needs, / Man's life is cheap as beast's."

Lear had believed that he could keep the symbols of power without bearing its burdens. In some ways, he is like those who claim that literature can have symbolic power without being responsibly engaged with the cares of the world. And if Lear resembles those artists who believe it possible for art to have power without responsibility, then Goneril and Regan may resemble those who claim that literature is a waste of time. When they mock their father about his need for "useless" symbols, they sound like the people who cannot understand why anyone would want to spend time reading poems and stories, instead of learning money-making skills. Lear's response is that all of us care deeply about symbolic things. Without our symbols, our lives would be "cheap as beast's," for in our power to make and comprehend symbols resides a good deal of our unique nature as *human* beings.

The arguments Goneril and Regan make against their father's need for symbols may seem familiar to anyone who knows the history of the Christian church. From prohibitions against images in the Old Testament to modern injunctions against ministerial robes, the church has struggled with the question of the place of visual images in its worship of the unseen God. In political movements sparked by the Reformation, for example, certain Christians destroyed stained glass in cathedrals and statues that depicted sacred scenes. Typical of such disdain for images is an observation by Nicholas Ridley, an Anglican bishop of London in the sixteenth century: "If by virtue of the second commandment, images were not lawful in the temple of the Jews, then by the same commandment they are not lawful in the churches of the Christians" (Pelikan, 4: 217).

Although Ridley's reasons for rejecting visual images are different from the reasons Goneril and Regan give for denying their father's requests concerning his knights, the bishop seems to share Lear's daughters' belief that truth is a matter of facts and has nothing to do with symbols. But that is a hard thing to claim consistently, for all of us take verbal and visual symbols seriously. If we object to the fact that a Lutheran minister or Episcopal priest wears a robe, what do we say about the fact that our own minister always wears a dark business suit? Is not the suit as much a symbol as the robe? Does it not *signify* a number of things about the values of its wearer and his culture?

Though we may choose not to read books, we cannot avoid "reading" our experiences to discover the meaning of the symbols we encounter and the stories we enact. Whenever we make a judgment about something, we engage in the act of interpreting. Many of our judgments seem to be matters of "common sense," because we reach them effortlessly and are convinced we could not possibly have made them differently. Yet even "common-sense" judgments are interpretations of a kind. The German philosopher Martin Heidegger explains:

> An interpretation is never a presuppositionless apprehending of something presented to us. If, when one is engaged in a particular concrete kind of interpretation, . . . one likes to appeal to what 'stands there,' then one finds that what 'stands there' in the first instance is nothing other than the obvious undiscussed assumption of the person who does the interpreting. (Heidegger, 191–92)

All of our knowledge relies upon such "undiscussed assumptions." For example, in recent decades, historians of science have come to speak of *paradigms,* which are basic pictures or models that scientists use to bring the facts of the physical world into a coherent whole. The Newtonian image of the world as a great mechanism was a powerful *paradigm.* For several centuries, that model of reality helped to explain many things about the created universe. If we could ask an educated person of the late eighteenth century to explain his or her *assumptions* about nature, we might well be met with laughter or confusion. At that point in history, Newton's theories seemed so conclusive that the average person would have been likely to consider the Newtonian model of reality to be a matter of common sense rather than an assumption of any kind. In the past century, however, following the work of Einstein and others, it has become much more difficult to argue that Newton's understanding of nature provides an exhaustive explanation of the created order.

Just as scientists use paradigms to organize their data, so do all of us use models to comprehend the world. Models enable students of the Scriptures to emphasize unifying themes as keys to the Bible and help political observers to put into perspective the events and trends of political life. Even infants are constantly about the business of organizing patterns of experience and expectation to help them interpret the many new things they encounter each day.

Paul Ricoeur argues that human actions are like books that stand in need of interpreters. "Like a text, human action is an open work, the meaning of which is 'in suspense,' " writes Ricoeur. "Human deeds are also waiting for fresh interpretations which decide their meaning. . . . Human action, too, is opened to anybody who *can read*" (*Hermeneutics*, 208). The understanding we acquire through reading of literature can help us make sense of human actions, just as an understanding of human behavior is essential for a deep appreciation of literature.

Reading Books

One of the most important ways that we can deepen our understanding of our world and actions is through a careful reading of books from the past—whether they be recognized classics or less familiar voices from that past. For the Christian, whose faith is rooted in the events of ancient Palestine and in the life of the Church and culture over the ages, history matters. "In life," writes Alasdair MacIntyre, "we are always under certain constraints. We enter upon a stage which we did not design and we find ourselves part of an action that was not our making" (213). To learn how to act in our present scene and to make sense of the stage we find ourselves upon, we explore the earlier scenes of our play as they have been recorded, in part, in the significant books that have come down to us from the past.

I began thinking in earnest about the classics when I taught junior and senior high-school English in the early 1970s. At that time I read a provocative book about "reading." It blamed teachers for forcing students to read the classics and claimed that most students were ill-suited for such books. It was not *what* they read that mattered, argued the author, but whether they read anything at all. He urged teachers to let students read anything they desired in the classroom, whether it was comic books, fan magazines, or the daily paper. At some point the students might move on to the classics, but in the meantime, at least they would be reading something.

Edmund Fuller, a distinguished Christian critic, must have had an argument such as this in mind when he wrote his final review column for the *Wall Street Journal:*

It has been argued that it is better for a person to read at any level of quality, even utter trash, than to read nothing. I'm not persuaded of that. A familiar saying, which never impressed me, is, "You are what you eat." Far more interestingly, as generalizations go: "You are what you read."

. . . [The printed word] gives us the extraordinary freedom to choose the intellectual company we will keep, to select those with whom, in spirit, we will walk. That is a privilege. Moreover, to those who can see it so, . . . in the highest sense it is a duty, in at least a due proportion of our reading time. Paraphrasing Joshua, 'Choose you this day whom you will read.' (34)

Drawing upon an image implicit in Fuller's comments, we might think of the history of literature as a great conversation. The writings of the past have shaped our present life and understanding, whether or not we realize it. Works such as the *Odyssey, Agamemnon,* Augustine's *Confessions,* the *Divine Comedy,* and the *Canterbury Tales* not only tell about distant realities but also uncover the origins of many present beliefs and practices. In addition, they may remind us of truths we have forgotten or bring to our attention truths we have never before confronted. In effect, such books are the only surviving "members" of the conversation that has gone into making us what we are.

Works from the past record truths and experiences that might otherwise have been lost. For example, in recent years some scholars have labored to bring back before our attention neglected master-pieces by women and ethnic minorities. As a result, works such as

Kate Chopin's *The Awakening* and the *Narrative of the Life of Frederick Douglass, an American Slave* can speak disturbing truths to us that otherwise we would not have heard.

To see how a classic from the past may help make sense of present experience, we can look briefly at one of the greatest American novels, Mark Twain's *The Adventures of Huckleberry Finn.* This novel about a boy's dramatic journey begins with young Huck letting everyone know how awful things have become for him in the home of the Widow Douglas. The Widow, who is "dismal regular and decent," wants to "learn" Huck about "Moses and the Bulrushers" and such stuff. Huck isn't interested, "because I don't take no stock in dead people." Caring little for the wisdom of the past, Huck wants a "free and easy" life away from the stifling rules of the Widow's world.

Because he cannot stand to be all "cramped up" and "civilized," Huck decides to stage his own "abduction" and "death." He escapes to an island on the Mississippi River, where he comes upon Jim, Miss Watson's runaway slave. At this point, Twain's central concern becomes the developing relationship between Huck and Jim. By fleeing down the river with Jim, Huck faces twin dangers. First, he puts himself at considerable risk by aiding a runaway slave. If discovered, Huck could face severe punishment. But more important for Twain is the danger Huck faces from his "conscience." The so-called conscience is Twain's ironic term for all the values of the slaveholding culture that have been drilled into Huck in his home, school, church, and village. Throughout his life, he has been told that the black man is inferior to the white man in every respect. But as he travels with Jim, Huck learns against his will that this black man is compassionate and, in many ways, better than any white person Huck has ever known.

Huck's conscience occasionally flares up and makes him feel guilty about his friendship with Jim. He is worried that it will "get all round, that Huck Finn helped a Nigger to get his freedom; and if I was to ever see anybody from that town again, I'd be ready to get down and lick his boots for shame." Finally, Huck writes to Miss Watson to turn Jim in:

> *Miss Watson your runaway nigger Jim is down here two mile below Pikes-ville and Mr. Phelps has got him and he will give him up for the reward if you send.*
>
> Huck Finn

I felt good and all washed clean of sin for the first time I had ever felt so in my life, and I knowed I could pray now. But I didn't do it straight off, but laid the paper down and set there thinking—thinking how good it was all this happened so, and how near I come to being lost and going to hell. And went on thinking. And got to thinking over our trip down the river; and I see Jim before me, all the time, in the day, and in the night-time, sometimes moonlight, sometimes storms, and we a-floating along, talking, and singing, and laughing. . . . And then I happened to look around, and see that paper.

It was a close place. I took it up, and held it in my hand. I was a-trembling, because I'd got to decide, forever, betwixt two things, and I knowed it. I studied a minute, sort of holding my breath, and then says to myself:

"All right, then, I'll *go* to hell"—and tore it up.

For some interpreters, Huck's defiant decision represents the triumph of the pure American heart over the corrupt practices of society. In later life, Twain wrote that *Huckleberry Finn* was "a book of mine where a sound heart and a deformed conscience come into collision and conscience suffers a defeat." By the "sound heart" Twain was referring to the "moral sense" of goodness and decency that he and others believed Americans possessed as an innate attribute. According to Twain, in the novel innate human goodness does battle with the "prejudices" that have made Huck—like his fellow citizens in a slaveholding society—a bad interpreter of human character and human action. According to this reading of the novel, goodness wins.

Huck's decision to "go to hell" has led other critics of the novel to an opposite conclusion. Huck's choice makes no ultimate difference, they say, for shortly after he makes it, he acquiesces to a

contorted scheme that Tom Sawyer concocts to free Jim from imprisonment on a southern farm. Huck stands back as Jim is treated
cruelly as an object of the white man's amusement. And Huck's
compassionate defiance ("All right, then, I'll *go* to hell") has no
power in the end. To resolve the plot, Twain had to rely upon the
conventions of the sentimental fiction he despised—the deathbed
"conversion," the fortunate secret will, and the like. Thus, the argument goes, Huck's "conversion" is of no consequence at all.

As Americans read this novel, many of them may be inclined to
admire Huck Finn. Because he embodies the youthful innocence, the
disdain for structure, and the deep skepticism about the past that
have been characteristic of American culture from its early stages, our
encounter with Huck may help us to discern vital truths about the
culture in which God has placed us. In a sense, as we watch Huck
develop, we are watching ourselves as we learn to read experiences
and books. In the America of Huck's time and in our time, it is easy
to believe that our "common-sense" assumptions are the natural
truth. Huck took it as a natural fact that the black person was inferior
to the white. We may assume other things to be obvious truths—
perhaps that all who are poor have chosen to be poor or that the past
is irrelevant to the promise and pressures of the present. One of the
most important things *Huckleberry Finn* can teach us is that we must
reassess our deep-seated assumptions. Such is the power that a great
book may have.

To conclude: we find ourselves drawn to read books, because for
human beings interpreting is as natural as breathing. Significant
books give us an unparalleled opportunity to hear from those who are
separated from us in time and space. They may either affirm or
challenge our deepest values. In reading the *Odyssey, Oedipus Rex,*
the *Divine Comedy,* and *King Lear,* we learn where we, as members
of a culture, have come from; in reading *The Grapes of Wrath, The
Waste Land,* and Sylvia Plath's poetry, we discover where we are; and
in reading *Invisible Man, A Bend in the River,* and *The Gulag
Archipelago,* we encounter visions of where we may be be going and
what we should and should not become.

In reading a worthwhile book, we may explore the mysteries and interpret the meaning of the world in which God has placed us. There are indeed other ways to go about gaining an understanding of oneself, God, and the world. But works of literature afford a special chance to enter into conversation with the great characters and interpreters of the human drama. In large measure, we read in order to learn the truth, which we may encounter in the pages of a book in powerful and convincing ways.

Chapter 2

THE LANGUAGE OF LITERATURE

Our birth is but a sleep and a forgetting.
> —WILLIAM WORDSWORTH, "Ode: Intimations of Immortality"

"When the Sun rises do you not see a round Disk of fire somewhat like a Guinea?" O no, no, I see an Innumerable company of the Heavenly host crying "Holy Holy Holy is the Lord God Almighty."
> —WILLIAM BLAKE, "A Vision of the Last Judgment"

> Now that my ladder's gone,
> I must lie down where all the ladders start,
> In the foul rag-and-bone shop of the heart.
> —WILLIAM BUTLER YEATS, "The Circus Animals' Desertion"

It is not difficult for us to recognize that novels, poems, and plays are set apart from other kinds of writing by their special use of language. Literary works take liberties with the facts, through their use of surprising metaphors or other extravagant figures of speech. In poems and stories, writers seem to do things with words that they couldn't or wouldn't do in other contexts. In the past century, some influential observers have gone so far as to speak of literature's use of a special language. According to them, literature involves the imaginative use of a language of metaphor and feeling and has special rights to this kind of language.

But for all those who are drawn to literature by the claim that it involves the use of a unique language, there are just as many who turn away from fiction and poetry because literary language seems esoteric and irrelevant to their lives. Indeed, many people will read books in general but will shy away from a specific book if they discover it is "literary." Often, such people argue that though it may be worthwhile to read something that provides useful information, it does not make sense to waste time reading works filled with metaphors, similes, and the like.

Stereotypes are at the heart of such a defense of literature and such complaints against it. The stereotypes have grown out of the belief that when we write or speak, we can use distinctly different types of language—a rational and scientific language, on the one hand, and an emotive and poetic language, on the other. According to these common conceptions, there are *proper* words, which express the truth in the form of facts, and *figurative* words, which express our feelings instead of reflecting things as they are. This distinction between proper and figurative language has a rich history in Western thinking and is the assumption behind many of our beliefs about the nature of language and literature.

As a consequence of this sharp distinction between two types of language, we in the modern world have developed a habit of separating metaphorical language (and the literature in which it appears) from what we consider "real life." We are inclined, it seems, to think of metaphors as a form of indulgence. They express deep feelings and strong desires, and those who enjoy them have a special need for the particular comforts and pleasures they provide. But as a means of describing or dealing with reality, figurative language is held to be woefully inadequate.

What these stereotypes of language do not acknowledge, however, is that all use of language is, in a genuine sense, metaphorical. Recent developments in the history of science and the philosophy of language have led to a reassessment of the sharp distinctions so long maintained between the languages of fact and feeling. Yet in spite of these developments in theories of language, changes in popular conceptions of metaphor have come slowly. In this chapter, we will consider some key challenges to the traditional view of metaphor and symbolic language. And in response to these challenges, this chapter will argue that the use of language in literature has more in common with our everyday practices than we may have realized. Of course, imaginative literature does make special use of metaphor, and we will examine one poet's development of the possibilities of metaphor. But at the same time, the chapter will explore how an understanding of metaphor's role in literature may deepen our awareness of its presence and functions in all uses of language.

Metaphor: A Brief History

It is possible to trace a skeptical view of metaphor back to the Greek philosopher Aristotle. In an influential work, Aristotle claims that metaphor "consists in giving the thing a name that belongs to something else" (1476). To see how little Western thinking about metaphor changed for centuries, we need only compare Aristotle's definition with the one given in the modern *Oxford English Dictionary*. That work describes metaphor as a "figure of speech in which a name or descriptive term is transferred to some object different from . . . that to which it is properly applicable." According to the modern dictionary and the ancient philosopher, specific words "belong" to specific things, and when we create a metaphor, we are "borrowing" a word from its proper "owner" to "lend" it to something else. This conception of metaphor implies that metaphors are abnormal. By "bumping" proper words out of their rightful places, metaphors seem to do deviant, unnatural things.

If metaphor falls short of the truth and does little real good, why should we bother with it at all? The answer Aristotle gave to that question became the standard one for centuries. In effect, he argued that we use metaphor to add appeal to an otherwise boring argument. "We ought in fairness to fight our case with no help beyond the bare facts," Aristotle states. "Still . . . other things affect the result considerably, owing to the defects of our hearers" (1435–36). Because of the inability of our audience, we add metaphors to what we say as a "seasoning of the meat." Metaphors are spices to flavor the truth or adornments to dress up an otherwise unappealing body of belief.

In one form or another, this view of metaphor has shaped our thinking for centuries. It holds that the real business of life occurs in a realm where words mean what they say and the facts are clear.

In *The Mirror and the Lamp,* M. H. Abrams describes the approach to metaphor taken by Thomas Sprat, the seventeenth-century British historian:

'Specious *Tropes and Figures* [images],' however justifiable in the past, ought now to be banished 'out of all *civil Societies,* as a thing fatal to Peace and good Manners.' Since they also bring 'mists and uncertainties on our knowledge,' the Royal Society has constantly resolved 'to return back to the primitive purity and shortness, when men deliver'd so many *things* almost in an equal number of *words'* and has exacted 'a close, naked, natural way of speaking . . . as near the Mathematical plainness as they can.' (285)

To have a plain and unadorned prose and to employ a "close, naked, natural way of speaking"—is it not ironic that a man who argues against metaphors finds himself talking about "mists" of knowledge, "primitive purity," and "naked" prose? Something is wrong here, and it is something that my children recognized when I read this passage while teaching an adult education class several years ago at a Chicago church. When I mentioned Sprat's reference to "naked" prose, my young son and daughter giggled audibly in the back row. Why did they laugh? Because they realized that there was something funny in the way the word "naked" had been used in that context. They were sensitive to the discrepancy between the common meaning and the figurative use of the word. Sprat thought he could be free of metaphor, but my children intuitively understood that our speech is never naked but always clothed in metaphorical figures.

What would happen to our view of metaphor if we were to discover that *proper* language was not really all that proper? In recent decades, repeated studies of the use of language in the sciences have revealed the presence of metaphor even in the most "factual" intellectual enterprises. It is time and familiarity that make words become "literal," the British writer Owen Barfield argues. "Literalness is a quality which some words have achieved in the course of their history. It is not a quality with which the first words were born" (55). Barfield is referring to the fact that the meanings of words evolve throughout the history of language. A word becomes literal over the course of time. The relationship between words and things is not a matter of nature, as though only certain words "belong" to certain things, but one of convention.

In an important work, *On Christian Doctrine*, St. Augustine describes the difference between *natural* and *conventional* signs. Natural signs are those which signify something unintentionally; smoke (as a sign of fire) and animal tracks (as a sign of a creature's presence and movement) are by this definition natural signs. Such signs are not a product of language, for fires and deer do not need words to make their marks. On the other hand, "conventional signs are those which living creatures show to one another for the purpose of conveying, in so far as they are able, the motion of their spirits or something which they have sensed or understood" (34–35). As an example of conventional signs, Augustine discusses the motions made by dancers in the theater of the ancient world:

If those signs which the actors make in their dances had a natural meaning and not a meaning dependent on the institution and consent of men, the public crier in early times would not have had to explain to the Carthaginian populace what the dancer wished to convey during the pantomime. (61)

The meaning of the dancers' performance depended upon an understanding of the conventional practices of society. According to Augustine, the relationship of words to things is dependent upon the customs and institutions that men and women have developed as creatures of culture. In modern terms, a similar point is often made by saying that the relationship between the signifier (the word we use to describe or "point to" a reality) and the signified (the reality described or pointed to by the word) always depends upon the decisions that have been made in the history of language.

Instead of seeing this belief—that the relationship of words to things is a matter of convention and not of nature—as proof of the random or arbitrary relationship of words to things, the Christian might argue that God creates the meaning of words along with the men and women to whom he has given the power to make history. The meaning of any word represents countless actions and decisions made throughout the history of a language, and a study of that history makes it very difficult to believe that words and things fit magically together. Rather, the history of words reveals that their meanings accumulate and shift over the years as part of the metaphorical process at work in all of language.

The Christian who is made uneasy by the thought that the meanings of words shift through the ages should consider the nature of Christian revelation. The full truth of the Scriptures was hardly given to Adam and Eve at creation. Nor was it even revealed fully to Noah, Abraham, or David. Instead, God chose to reveal his will gradually. Abraham was given a promise ("I will make you into a great nation"), and a Christian might argue that it was not until the appearance of Jesus that the nature of that promise became fully apparent. And even now, after two thousand years of Christian history, we continue to dwell upon the mysteries hidden in Christ. Though Christ is the same yesterday, today, and forever, who would dare say that our understanding of him never grows or changes?

Furthermore, the fact that the meanings of words change over time is nicely illustrated by the history of the word *cross* in the Judeo-Christian tradition. In the English language, the literal meaning of this word seems unmistakable. The cross is the pole-like structure on which Christ was crucified, and the word's significance seems clear even to many who do not believe in the Gospel. A study of the *Oxford English Dictionary* reveals that specific Christian associations were present in the word from its earliest appearance in the English language.

It is another matter, however, when we consider the origins of the word in the Greek language of the New Testament. The two words translated as *cross* in English are *xylon* and *stauros* in Greek, and before the crucifixion of Jesus both words pointed primarily to the shame and degradation associated with crucifixion in the ancient world. Though Jewish law did not itself impose crucifixion, Judaism did consider crucifixion to be a shameful way to die; a man hanged on a tree was accursed in the sight of God (Deuteronomy 21:23). The Christian, however, will find in the word *cross* associations that would have shocked a person from the Old Testament and the ancient world. According to the Apostle Paul, "Christ redeemed us from the curse of the law by becoming a curse for us, for it is written: 'Cursed is everyone who is hung on a tree' " (Galatians 3:13). And in another context Paul argues that though Christ crucified is "a stumbling block to Jews and foolishness to Gentiles," he remains "the power of God and the wisdom of God" to those who have heard his call (1 Corinthians 1:23–24). In the providence of God, the Christian student of language could say, the Apostle Paul brought the word *cross* into a rich interaction with common words such as *freedom*, *forgiveness*, *power*, and *glory*. From the process, the word *cross* emerged with dramatically different, rich, and authoritative meanings which would have profound significance for Christians through the ages.

The contemporary theologian Helmut Thielicke has sought to explain in general terms the metaphorical process by means of which the New Testament appropriates or "baptizes" words from pagan and Jewish contexts. Terms such as *Logos, Messiah,* and *Son of Man* are "impressed into service" in the New Testament, and "their meaning changes." But this change in meaning is not total. "If it were, the terms could be used at random and filled with any content. This is not so. They have from the outset some affinity to the content in whose service they are put." It is possible to describe this affinity and change, Thielicke claims,

by saying that when the words enter the NT they are baptized; a new creation is made of them; the 'old' of their former content has passed away. Yet in spite of this surrender of identity as a new creation, their former existence continues as in baptism. This is an indication that the choice of words for what has to be expressed in revelation is not haphazard. (79)

Though the most important terms in the life of the Christian are not natural symbols of some spiritual reality, Thielicke is arguing, the words that the writers of scripture employ have associations that make it logical to use them in a new context to describe the saving action of God in Christ.

This discussion of the history of changes in our language, and in specific Christian uses of language, has brought us to a point where a redefinition of metaphor is in order. In place of the long-standing Aristotelian view of metaphor as *substitution,* as a process in which poetic words "stand in" for literal ones, we could perhaps say that the metaphorical process is one of *interaction.* When we use a metaphor, *we say that one thing is another.* We take a word from its conventional context and apply it to a new situation. To make a metaphor is to say that "a mighty fortress is our God," that the two tallest players on the University of Kentucky basketball team were "twin towers" who had a hard time putting the "rock" through the "hoop," or that "television is chewing gum for the eyes." Since we all are always saying that one thing is another, we are all, in a real sense, "masters of metaphor" (Aristotle's phrase).

If we think of metaphor in this way, we see that metaphors are relished by almost all who are capable of human speech. If making a metaphor involves "saying that one thing is another," rather than "substituting" a false but pleasing image for a literal but unsatisfying word, then we see that metaphorical process is at the heart of all our knowing. We acquire information, we organize what we know, and we make innovative breakthroughs through the use of metaphor.

For example, take the fact that I am typing my chapters in this book on a Macintosh computer. You might say that the Macintosh program is one big metaphor. Many people refer to the Macintosh as "user-friendly"; what they mean is that it employs metaphors with which we are familiar and comfortable. Those of you who have seen a Macintosh at work realize that when you insert a *disk,* a *desktop* appears on the monitor; on the *desktop* appears at least one, and perhaps more, *window;* in a *window* you see *folders,* inside which you can find the *documents* you've been working on. And as would be the case with any decent *desktop,* you have alongside your desk a *trash-*can into which you can dump unwanted *documents.*

The people at Apple Computer have done what all of us are always doing to make sense of our lives and the many new experiences in them. They have tried to use metaphors to make the alien world of computing less intimidating. In the interaction between our familiar world of files, windows, desktops, and trash cans and the pictures on a Macintosh screen, we encounter the process by means of which we are constantly assessing and appropriating new information. Without metaphor, we would never feel at home in our "familiar" world, nor would we be able to come to terms with alien realities.

In his introduction to poetry, *Western Wind*, the poet and critic John Frederick Nims relates a story in order to make a corresponding point about simile, which is a metaphorical comparison using *like* or *as:*

> Our effort to understand anything starts by relating it to something better known which it resembles. . . . [In 1971] two of our astronauts, working in moondust which they had never seen before, could use nothing but *like's* to describe it:
> "When you put your scoop in, it smooths it out—just *like* plaster."
> "I was going to say—*like* cement. . . .
> The mind operates by finding likenesses. When a new piece of information is fed into the brain, it is whirled around the circuits until it finds its place with similar things. Otherwise we would not only learn nothing; we would not even long survive in a world full of hazards we have to identify. (19–20)

This fact—that metaphor is at the heart of all knowledge—means that the person who studies literature ought not to believe that he or she is engaged in an esoteric activity; nor should that person feel guilty that the appreciation of metaphor is a diversion from the "real business" of life.

Poets and critics do not engage in an exclusive activity when they deal with metaphors. The difference between a poet and the rest of us is that the poet uses figurative language more self-consciously and skillfully than we do. Many of us can play tennis, beat out a tune on the piano, or wield a hammer to install a cabinet. But only a few of us have the skill to do those things very well. The same is true for the poet, who does brilliantly what we do unconsciously in our own halting ways every day.

Poetry: Metaphor at Work

Though it would be unwise to claim that the poet's use of language is entirely different from our own, poetry does involve a more self-conscious use of figurative language than is common in everyday speech or writing. Though all of us use metaphor, not all of us, by any reasonable definition, are poets.

To see what a specific poet and poem can do with metaphor, we can turn again to a work by Emily Dickinson. A gifted creator of metaphors, Dickinson offers us a surprising view of death in her poem, "What Inn is this?":

> What Inn is this
> Where for the night
> Peculiar Traveller comes?
> Who is the Landlord?
> Where the maids?
> Behold, what curious rooms!
> No ruddy fires on the hearth—
> No brimming Tankards flow—
> Necromancer! Landlord!
> Who are these below?

I said earlier in this chapter that we use metaphor to make that which is alien seem familiar; in other words, we often use metaphor in an attempt to come to terms with new and potentially frightening realities. In "What Inn is this?" we watch this process at work. As the poem opens, we seem to ask the question along with the narrator: What kind of place is this? The speaker is at the end of a day's journey and is looking for a place for the night. We are as mystified as she is about the place she has come to. *Where* is it? *What* is it? "Who is the Landlord?" "Where the maids?"

The situation offers the speaker no immediate answers to her questions. Indeed there is no activity at all in this inn; there are "No ruddy fires on the hearth—/ No brimming Tankards flow." This is certainly a strange inn with such "curious rooms." It is a place marked by the absence of those things we associate with the life of an inn, or we might say, that we associate with life itself. And only in the final two lines do we begin to get a clear idea of our surroundings: "Necromancer! Landlord!/ Who are these below?" A necromancer is one who conjures "the spirits of the dead for purposes of magically revealing the future." The root of the word is the Greek word *nekros*, meaning "dead body."

"So, that is it!" we think, as we realize that the inn is a crypt or tomb, and the silent guests are the ageless dead. After all, we may conclude, life is a "journey" at the end of which we anticipate a rest at "night" (Hebrews 4). But is this the kind of place we anticipated? This is not the comforting image we had in mind of eternal rest. Nor is this even a typical inn. The eighteenth- or nineteenth-century tavern had a blazing fire and convivial talk, but this inn is a frighteningly quiet place. And heaven for Dickinson's Christian audience would have been associated with bliss and security, rather than the eerie realities of this poem.

The central metaphor of the poem is that the crypt is an inn, or something to that effect. The metaphor makes a foreign reality—the actual state of the dead—something we can grasp through a familiar association. In the interaction between death (or crypt) and inn, an exchange of qualities takes place. The crypt takes on some of the traits of an inn, but at the same time, this particular inn seems strangely like a crypt in its silence and its lack of any sign of life.

Thus, it is not correct to say that in the making of metaphors one figurative word is merely substituted for a literal word whose meaning is perfectly clear to us. The transaction is too rich and complex for such a simple explanation. What happens is that the two distinct worlds of inn and tomb are brought together, and in the process we see the strange made familiar and the familiar made eerily strange.

As the process by which that which is strange and unknown is made familiar, metaphor serves as a primary means by which we make intellectual discoveries. Through metaphors, we can see similarities and possibilities we never before imagined. To have said that the universe is a vast and complex machine (as many who came after

Isaac Newton claimed), for example, was to have made a revolutionary statement. In the late twentieth century, we continue to live with the implications of this shift from the medieval metaphor of organic harmony to the early modern image of the world as a realm of mechanism and law. Metaphors matter.

The philosopher Max Black uses a specific recent example to demonstrate the significance of this view of metaphor as a means of making revolutionary discoveries. "Did genes exist before their existence was recognized by biologists?" Black asks. His answer is "Yes and No." Genes did exist insofar as they were not created out of nothing by men and women. But, Black argues, "it is less obvious that *genes* 'were there all the time, waiting to be discovered.' The term 'gene' has its place within a man-made theory, in whose absence it would have no intelligible use." The elements of germ plasm we call "genes" obviously existed before biologists discovered and named them; but in a very real sense, the physical properties we have labeled with the metaphor "genes" did not appear until a particular biological model (an extended metaphor) "drew them out." Thus, in Black's words, "some metaphors are . . . indispensable for perceiving connections that, once perceived, are then truly present" (38–39).

If it is true that the poet "uses figurative language in a more self-conscious and skillful manner than we do," then one justification for the study of literature is that it offers us excellent examples of this vital activity. In the metaphors of a poem we may discover a new possibility for our understanding of ourselves, nature, or God. The metaphorical imagination "contributes concretely . . . to the *projection* of new possibilities of describing the world," Paul Ricoeur argues ("The Metaphorical Process," 152).

Since making a metaphor involves "saying that one thing is another," well-wrought metaphors give us a glimpse of what it would be like to live in a world where everything makes sense and holds together. When we we say that one thing is another, we are saying that though the two are not identical, they are related. And in saying that, we are implying that the world just might be a place of ultimate meaning and mystery. The Christian believes in God's ultimate, ordered rule; effective metaphors give us a hint of that order.

Thus, to say that one thing is another is both to deepen our understanding of what we already know and to add to our knowledge things we had never before imagined. When we deal in metaphors, we are dealing with the very stuff of intelligent life. We find metaphors not only in the pages of poetry anthologies, but also in the advertisements we read, in the sermons we hear, and in the pleasant and passionate statements we make to one another. We are unwise if we believe that we can go beyond metaphor in our use of language, or that we need to do so; we are wise if we learn to create and comprehend metaphors with skill and delight. To become a "master of metaphor" is, in many ways, to become a master of understanding.

Chapter 3

THE PLACE OF STORIES

An eminent physicist, Steven Weinberg, recently discussed whether or not the universe has a beginning and end. What he said about that question may be of interest to Christians who consider the matter of storytelling. Weinberg explained that he would like to believe that there is a *meaningful* story to be told about the universe. But he concluded that any such story could be nothing but the product of wish fulfillment:

It is almost irresistible for humans to believe that we have some special relation to the universe, that human life is not just a more-or-less farcical outcome of a chain of accidents reaching back to the first three minutes, but that we were somehow built in from the beginning. . . . It is very hard to realize that this all [the earth] is just a tiny part of an overwhelmingly hostile universe. It is even harder to realize that this present universe has evolved from an unspeakably unfamiliar early condition, and faces a future extinction of endless cold or intolerable heat. The more the universe seems comprehensible, the more it also seems pointless. (McFarland, 200)

The dilemma facing this distinguished scientist seems to be a common one for educated men and women of our day. Weinberg wants to believe ("it is almost irresistible") that human life fits into a grand and meaningful story that can be told about the created universe. It is too painful to assume that human life is the "more-or-less farcical outcome of a chain of accidents." But even though all of us long to believe in a glorious destiny for ourselves and our world, Weinberg believes we must resign ourselves to the fact that our world "faces a future extinction of endless cold or intolerable heat." A naive person may believe that life has a purposeful goal, but the more the educated person understands about the universe, "the more it seems pointless."

For almost two thousand years, Christians have believed their universe to be anything but pointless. They have been convinced that the stories they tell about its origin and destiny correspond to reality. For example, in writing of his pilgrimage through hell, purgatory, and heaven, Dante undoubtedly believed that his story described the true state of things. In writing about these realms, Dante was not just referring to his own hopes and fears; rather, he believed himself to be depicting the way things ultimately were. That is not to say that he believed in the literal reality of each punishment he envisioned in hell or in the existence of each of the levels on the way to the Blessed Vision of Paradise. He knew that his story could offer nothing more than an approximation of the ultimate truth, but it pointed to that truth nonetheless. For Dante and others of his age, stories and realities did fit together.

Obviously, something dramatic took place in the relationship between stories and reality in the period between the medieval poet Dante and the contemporary scientist Steven Weinberg. It will be the purpose of this chapter, in part, to consider what happened in that change. Of equal importance, however, will be our attempts to recapture some sense of the positive power of stories. The narratives we encounter in epic poems, in plays, and in novels are anything but fanciful alternatives to real life. The fact is that we never get away from stories. In and out of literature, stories tell us who we are and what we might become.

Story's History

As was true of metaphor, so is it true of stories that we can trace many of our ideas back to Aristotle. In the *Poetics*, Aristotle defined tragedy as "an imitation of an action that is complete in itself." It is a "whole" which "has beginning, middle, and end" (1462). Aristotle claimed that tragedy imitated human action by selecting out the most important characteristics of that action. For Aristotle, to imitate nature and human action did not mean to copy them, but to re-present them in a thorough and fair manner. According to Aristotle, tragic stories did this work of selecting and elevating better than any other form of writing. And in displaying the universal elements of human experience, Aristotle believed, tragedy did not impose an arbitrary form on human experience. Instead, it drew out the deep patterns already present in that experience.

As important as Aristotle may have been, however, his influence on our Western understanding of "story" pales in comparison to that of the Bible. The Old and New Testaments tell a sweeping tale that encompasses all of human history and experience. The Great Beginning of all things is depicted in Genesis; the climactic end of creation is foretold in Revelation; in between this Beginning and End, we encounter individual stories of conflict and resolution, we discover the source of conflict in sin, and we learn of the One who came to overcome sin. The Bible claims to do nothing less than offer the definitive explanation of the origin and destiny of all things.

Over the centuries, the biblical narrative exercised a dramatic influence on the shape of the stories told by the writers of the Western World. The world of classical antiquity viewed history as either a decline from a primitive grandeur or as a series of cyclical developments—from better to worse, and back to better again. With the advent of Christianity, however, Western views of history changed dramatically. Cyclical views were replaced by linear views; that is, it became possible to think of history as having a clear origin, shape, and end. "As against Greco-Roman views, the Christian pattern of history . . . is finite; it has a clearly defined plot; [and] it is providential" (Abrams, *Natural Supernaturalism*, 35). Thus, the Western understanding of stories developed largely under the significant influence of the biblical narrative. Like the Bible, stories as we have come to think of them have distinct beginnings and endings; they contain conflicts and work their way through to resolutions of one kind or another.

But what can be the role of such stories in the modern world, if many contemporary men and women no longer believe, as the scientist quoted at the beginning of this chapter no longer believes, that the world has a clear beginning or a meaningful end? If stories cannot point to an ultimate order, what can they do? In the past two hundred years, perhaps the most common answer to that question has been that, regardless of their truthfulness, coherent stories may satisfy our desires for the appearance of meaning and order.

In *Natural Supernaturalism*, M. H. Abrams outlines the process by which the writers of the Romantic age (at the beginning of the nineteenth century) set out to salvage the Christian story. They sought to do so by making the Bible an illustration of the drama of the individual soul's struggles rather than claiming it to be a description of the actual course of history. "History is an impertinence and an injury," the American Ralph Waldo Emerson wrote, "if it be any thing more than a cheerful apologue or parable of my being and becoming."

While the romantic poets and novelists had a tendency to turn the biblical drama into an illustration of the struggles of the individual soul, other post-Christian movements have also borrowed heavily from the biblical view of history. The faith in progress that has characterized Western life in recent centuries is in large measure a legacy of biblical conceptions of history and hope. And as many observers have pointed out, Marxism is deeply indebted to Christianity for its prophetic images of the redemption of history. As the Christian philosopher Karl Löwith explains, modern thinkers may have rejected historic Christian belief, but they have maintained a Christian *faith* in the future: "Transformed into a secular theory of progress, the scheme of the history of salvation could seem to be natural and demonstrable" (186).

Among scholars of literature in recent decades, however, perhaps the most common defense of stories has been based upon the claim that they are vital because they satisfy fundamental human needs. According to the contemporary critic Frank Kermode, "right down at the root, they [fictions] must correspond to a basic human need, they must make sense, give comfort" (44). We should note the dramatic difference between Kermode's observation and what was said earlier about Dante. In Dante's world, a story about the terrors of hell and the bliss of heaven corresponded to reality. Such a story described, however inadequately, the ultimate state of things. But in the modern vision, as Kermode describes it, stories correspond to our needs and not to a reality beyond them. The story-teller and reader must remember that the comforts of stories have no bearing upon the hard facts of reality. According to the view that Kermode represents, we can find delight and solace between the covers of a book, but we should never mistake the attractive vision we find there for the facts about life.

A problem with this view, as with the perspective offered in Steven Weinberg's understanding, is that it grants too great authority to a naive conception of "facts." It seems to assume that a fact is an isolated piece of information that makes sense on its own, independent of any larger framework. "Fact," writes Alasdair MacIntyre in *After Virtue*, "is in modern culture a folk-concept with an aristocratic ancestry" (78). To put our modern understanding of "fact" into perspective, he offers the example of a modern person who gazes into the night sky and sees stars and planets. In looking at the same scene, a medieval observer might have claimed to see not stars and planets but "chinks in a sphere through which the light beyond could be observed" (79). Which observer—the medieval or modern—has represented the facts of the heavens accurately? A modern scientist might claim that what both saw were "small light patches against a dark surface." These would supposedly be the facts, by a strict scientific definition. But a world in which physical descriptions are reduced to records of random sensations is a meaningless world, MacIntyre argues: "if all our experience were to be characterised exclusively in terms of this bare sensory type of description . . . we would be confronted with . . . an uninterpretable world" (79).

Interestingly enough, our modern worship of facts has coincided with the decline of the influence of the Christian story on the Western mind. In the medieval and early modern worlds, questions of ends dominated thinking about the nature of events and objects. To understand something, one had to know the purpose for which it had been created. For several centuries, however, the emphasis has been shifting from questions of ends to questions of origin. When we seek to explain something, we are no longer likely to ask, "What was the end for which this object has been created?" but "What was its source?" To understand something, we tend to want to learn where it has come from and how it works; we think of facts as items to be calculated or explained to help us understand how things have developed.

It is easy to forget that the mechanistic model which gave birth to the concept of fact was in itself a part of a larger "story." Those who worship facts have overlooked the fact that facts make sense only when they fit into some form of coherent story. That is, we never know anything in isolation, but only in context. In our actions and practices, we are story-telling creatures, MacIntyre argues:

> We enter human society, that is, with one or more imputed characters—roles into which we have been drafted—and we have to learn what they are in order to be able to understand how others respond to us and how our responses to them are apt to be construed. . . . Deprive children of stories and you leave them unscripted, anxious stutterers in their actions as in their words. (216)

MacIntyre's observations have significant implications for an understanding of literature. The previous chapter argued that metaphor is at the heart of the process by which we come to know anything. It is possible to make similar claims for stories. If they are fundamental to the way we organize and understand our world, then the works of dramatists, short story writers, and novelists should be seen as vital instances of a universal activity. To tell a story involves more than indulging a need for amusement or providing an outlet for a stifled imagination. The authors of *Habits of the Heart,* a recent study of American culture and values, claim that "what we need from history, is . . . some idea of how we have gotten from the past to the present, in short, a narrative. Narrative is a primary and powerful way by which to know about a whole. In an important sense, what a society (or a person) is, is its history" (Bellah et al., 302). Through the telling of stories, we struggle to discover what we have been, who we are, and what we ought to be.

There are, of course, significant differences between the stories that a writer of history tells and the stories that a dramatist or novelist creates. Even while acknowledging the presence of a creative element in all stories, the historian argues that his or her work is faithful to the events of the past. The writer of a work of imaginative literature, however, is not bound to represent actual events. Instead, he or she is free to imagine what might have happened or what might still occur. The critic Clarence Walhout has argued that works of fiction serve as models through which "we explore the possibilities of understanding and living in the world." They "open up for us new ways of reflecting on the world" (Lundin, 59).

The world of the fictional story is like our world yet distinct from it. If we read a novel by Jane Austen—or watch a movie by Steven Spielberg, for that matter—we have no trouble realizing that the characters we meet and the scenes they enact are "made up." Yet, at the same time, we recognize our world and our acquaintances in the imaginary realm of the novel or movie. The work of fiction makes enough contact with our everyday lives to make sense to us, and is also different enough to challenge us to think of new ways of understanding the meaning and course of our actions. Fiction illuminates our lives, just as our lived experience helps us to make sense of the stories we read.

As modern individualists, we are prone to think of ourselves as masters of our own stories. But in reality, as the poet and essayist Wendell Berry wrote recently,

The problem, of course, is that we are *not* the authors of ourselves. That we are not is a religious perception, but it is also a biological and a social one. Each of us has had many authors, and each of us is engaged, for better or worse in that same authorship. We could say that the human race is a great coauthorship in which we are collaborating with God and nature in the making of ourselves and one another. From this there is no escape. (115)

"The notion that one discovers one's deepest beliefs in, and through, tradition and community is not very congenial to Americans," we read in *Habits of the Heart,* but the truth is that "we find ourselves not independently of other people and institutions but through them." Along with the Victorian poet William Henley, each of us may desire to assert, "I am the master of my fate; / I am the captain of my soul" ("Invictus"). Yet the fact remains that there is much in our lives that "we do not control, that we are not even 'responsible' for, that we receive as grace or face as tragedy, things Americans habitually prefer not to think about" (Bellah et al., 84).

To a group of early Christians, the writer of the book of Hebrews presents a history of the faithfulness of God and his people. It is the history into which the early Christian church was born, so to speak. The author of Hebrews challenges his readers to remember the great figures of Israel's past, those men and women whose faith should encourage those who now worship God through the person of Jesus Christ. The people of the Old Testament lived by faith, the author says, and they never entered fully "upon the promised inheritance." In other words, the story of God's involvement with humanity did not end with the Israelites, "because, with us in mind, God had made a better plan, that only in company with us should they reach their perfection" (Hebrews 11:40, New English Bible). The Bible commands us to think of our individual dramas as being set within a larger story of past faithfulness, present rule, and promise for the future.

A Story of the New World

To understand both the importance of stories and several key American assumptions about their role in our lives, we can consider a well-known American story, *The Autobiography of Benjamin Franklin.* Franklin is an excellent representative of the modern scientific tradition and its celebration of "facts." He had great confidence in his ability to discover the truth through a study of the facts of nature and history and was an eloquent spokesman for that American tradition which scorns tradition. Franklin would have disagreed with many of the writers I have cited in this chapter. What mattered for him was not so much the story an American was born into, but the story that the American could create for his or her own life.

Yet like every other human being, Benjamin Franklin was born into a very specific story. Puritan beliefs shaped the life of the family and the community in which he was raised. The Christian saga of redemption and the American tale of flight from persecution formed the background for his world, but it is intriguing to see how Franklin rewrote these stories. He took the sagas of sin, divine grace, redemption, and communal life and transformed them into tales about the triumph of the individual in the vast expanses of the New World.

For example, Franklin's account of his arrival in Philadelphia in 1723 follows a pattern established by early Puritan narratives, but makes several dramatic changes. In the *Autobiography*, Franklin tells how, having fled from apprenticeship to his brother in Boston, he arrived in Philadelphia owning little more than the clothes on his back and the pennies in his pocket. He purchased "three great Puffy Rolls" and strode down the street "with a Roll under each Arm, and eating the other." He gave two of his rolls to a woman and child who had come down river in the boat with him. Then, refreshed yet tired from the journey,

> I walk'd again up the Street, which by this time had many clean dress'd People in it who were all walking the same Way; I join'd them, and thereby was led into the great Meeting House of the Quakers near the Market. I sat down among them, and after looking round a while and hearing nothing said, being very drowsy thro' Labour and want of Rest the preceding Night, I fell fast asleep, and continu'd so till the Meeting broke up, when one was kind enough to rouse me. This was therefore the first House I was in or slept in, in Philadelphia.

There are many important similarities between this and another famous story from early American life. I am referring to the description William Bradford gives in *Of Plymouth Plantation* of the arrival of the Pilgrims in the new world in 1620. "Being thus passed the vast ocean," Bradford writes,

and a sea of troubles before in their preparation (as may be remembered by
that which went before), they had now no friends to welcome them nor inns
to entertain or refresh their weatherbeaten bodies; no houses or much less
towns to repair to, to seek for succor. . . . Besides, what could they see but
a hideous and desolate wilderness, full of wild beasts and wild men—and
what multitudes there might be of them they knew not.

Franklin's account of his arrival in Philadelphia echoes Bradford's
telling of the Puritan tale, but with significant differences. Bradford's
story is about a group of pilgrims entering a strange wilderness;
Franklin tells of an individual courageously moving to an alien city.
Bradford's pilgrims face life-threatening dangers of starvation, disease, and Indian attack, while Franklin's foe is the more ill-defined
fear of failure in a new place. The Pilgrims of Bradford's tale attribute
their success to their own courage and the grace of God; in Philadelphia, Ben Franklin succeeds through his ingenuity and stringent
self-discipline.

Ironically, Benjamin Franklin, who had a love of "facts" and
sought to be free of the power of past stories, was to become a source
of one of America's most compelling stories. He and others in the
eighteenth century reworked the Puritan story of a God-fearing community into a new tale about the self-made individual. In the middle
of his autobiography, Franklin inserted letters from two friends who
had encouraged him to complete the story of his life. Both urged him
to tell his readers how Americans can "write the stories" of their own
lives free of the burdensome influence of past stories. Franklin's
autobiography could prove truly useful, his friends believed, for his
story could promote a great "Spirit of Industry and early Attention
to Business, Frugality and Temperance with the American Youth."

A careful reader may note that, unlike his Puritan ancestors, Franklin makes few references to the Scriptures or classical texts. When
William Bradford or Jonathan Edwards sat down to compose a story
of the Puritan experience, they instinctively employed the Scriptures
and other resources from the classical past to make sense of it. For
the Puritan writers, the struggles of the individual could make sense
only in the larger dramas of the history of the church and God's

redemptive plan. Franklin, on the other hand, set out to write a story in which the relevance of the past would be downplayed or denied.

Franklin's relation to stories may remind us of Thomas Sprat's attitude towards metaphor. That commonsensical Englishman wanted to plant his feet on firm ground and to employ a "close, naked, natural way of speaking" but found himself caught by the undertow of metaphors anyway. Likewise, it seems ironic that although Franklin set out to deny the hold of past stories upon present actions, he wrote a narrative that strongly influenced future generations. Thus it is that while wishing to be free of the past and its restraints, Americans retell stories that proclaim their freedom from stories. The stories Americans tell themselves about the past are often about the great men and women who have struggled to release themselves from bondage to the past. In American culture, the disdain for tradition becomes a tradition in itself; the image of the man fighting to be free of the influence of others becomes an influential model for later generations; the story of the self-reliant individual becomes the shared vision of a culture.

The example of Franklin and his influence indicates that no matter how much we may long to move beyond the confines of stories, we find ourselves planted in the midst of them. For the Christian, this is especially true. The Bible is the great story book from beginning to end, Alpha to Omega. Our lives are framed within a story whose beginnings precede us by countless years and whose ends will not be told until that day when God is "all in all." Even when we cannot decipher the meaning of things we do and things that happen to us, we are guided by our trust that all things make ultimate sense. God is sovereign over all of history and over each of our lives.

Thus, in faith, the Christian can challenge the claim made by Steven Weinberg that the whole universe is "a more-or-less farcical outcome of a chain of accidents" and that it "faces a future extinction of endless cold or intolerable heat." For the Christian, there is a deep legitimacy to the stories we tell ourselves about the purposeful origins and meaningful ends of human life. Grounded in the conviction that the Creation is the ordered work of a loving God and that the Bible tells the grand story of all things, we may see the stories we create—in literature or films, for examples—as mirrors held up to that order.

Yes, the Christian can acknowledge, the stories we tell point to the desires of our hearts as well as to the realities of our world, but this does not mean what Weinberg and others might take it to mean. To him, our desire to believe in meaningful origins and ends is a sign of weakness; it shows our inability to come to terms with the fact that "the more the universe seems comprehensible, the more it also seems pointless." But for the Christian there need not be such a rigid dichotomy between desires and realities. In a sermon preached almost half a century ago, C. S. Lewis attacked this rigid separation:

We are told to deny ourselves and to take up our crosses in order that we may follow Christ; and nearly every description of what we shall ultimately find if we do so contains an appeal to desire. If there lurks in most modern minds the notion that to desire our own good and earnestly to hope for the enjoyment of it is a bad thing, I submit that this notion has crept in from Kant and the Stoics and is no part of the Christian faith. Indeed, if we consider the unblushing promises of reward and the staggering nature of the rewards promised in the Gospels, it would seem that Our Lord finds our desires not too strong, but too weak. (*Weight of Glory,* 3–4)

As we write the stories of our own lives through our choices and actions, we never know the full implications of what we have done. We do not know all the influences that went into any specific decision, nor can we predict all the consequences of any single action. We are to our own lives what authors are to the books they write, as the modern critic Mikhail Bakhtin repeatedly observed. Though we have considerable control over the stories we write, we can never grasp their full meaning. Our individual stories are part of a much larger story, which we glimpse in outline but not in full detail. For, "now we see but a poor reflection; then we shall see face to face. Now I know in part; then I shall know fully, even as I am fully known" (1 Corinthians 13:12).

Chapter 4

READING AND THE CHRISTIAN VOCATION

W ho was the first person to climb Mt. Everest, the highest mountain in the world? Although most histories credit Sir Edmund Hillary and the Sherpa Norgay Tengzing with achieving the first ascent in 1954, many climbers believe that another Englishman, George Mallory, reached the top of Everest in 1924 before disappearing from the north face of the Himalayan giant. His body has never been found, and climbing historians continue to debate the issue.

Although you may never have heard of Mallory, you probably are familiar with his famous reply to a reporter's question of why he was trying to climb Mt. Everest: "Because it's there." A recent biography (Holzel and Salkeld) claims that the entire incident is apocryphal, but other accounts of Mallory's life suggest that he felt it was impossible to explain his complex motivations for climbing and responded flippantly, "Because it's there," in order to squash the reporter's curiosity with a vague response.

These three words, whether actually spoken or not, have become a legend of mountaineering. For years, climbers have seen Mallory as aggressive and domineering, a man who had to accept, meet, and conquer every challenge. Thus interpreted, his words became a rallying cry for many mountaineers.

The stories behind the legendary words "Because it's there" demonstrate our natural tendency to engage in interpretation, to create narratives, and to use metaphor. But Mallory's words also provide a way for us to begin thinking about how we live our lives, and how literature relates to our existence.

Many people view their lives, whether they climb mountains or not, in terms similar to Mallory's. Some are casual: "Why worry about it? We are just here." Others are aggressive. Like the mythical challenge-meeting mountaineer, they want to conquer their surroundings and become like God. But neither a casual passivity nor an aggressive dominance provides a satisfactory rationale for our lives. We must explore the possibilities further, even as mountaineering historians must go beyond Mallory's words and popular interpretation of them to uncover his complex motivation for pursuing Mt. Everest.

Christians believe that historical existence has special meaning. We are the children of God, specially created by him and specially endowed with responsibilities. Our foremost duties are to acknowledge God, to call upon him for salvation through Christ, and to honor and serve him. The responsibility to serve God suggests that we must do more with our time on the earth than just wait to go to heaven. Too often we secure our salvation and then focus our energies on establishing a personally comfortable way of life. The Bible teaches, however, that we should carry out our responsibility to God by working to establish a world that would please and praise him. In so doing, we demonstrate our love and obedience to God as well as our love and care for our neighbor.

It may initially seem strange to say so, but reading literature is one way that we can attempt to carry out these responsibilities. The ability to write and read literature is a gift from God. Of all God's created beings, only human beings employ metaphors, narratives, and written communication. God not only gave humans these good gifts but also chose to reveal himself in part through a written text full of metaphors and narratives, the Bible. Because black marks on a white page can convey meaning, they can provide ways to interact with the world. Reading literature can thus help us as we attempt to understand and act in God's world.

The Christian Vocation

The Psalms discuss the special identity and responsibility of human beings within the creation:

> When I consider your heavens,
>   the work of your fingers,
> the moon and the stars,
>   which you have set in place,
> what is man that you are mindful of him?
>   the son of man that you care for him?
> You made him a little lower than the heavenly beings
>   and crowned him with glory and honor.
> You made him ruler over the works of your hands;
>   you put everything under his feet:
> all flocks and herds,
>   and the beasts of the field,
> the birds of the air,
>   and the fish of the sea,
>   all that swim the paths of the seas. (Psalm 8:3–8)

Next to the wonders of the heavens, we may feel small and insignificant. Yet God made us the crown of creation, formed in God's image and given magnificence and respect. As part of this special identity, we have been given a vocation. We are responsible for ruling the works of God's hands.

Some Christians have taken this vocation as a license to pillage and plunder the bounties of creation, but those who thoughtlessly exploit creation "because it's there" are not responsible rulers. What would we think of a King and Queen who descend upon their domain in order to seize all the food, strip the villagers of their possessions, take the wooden cottages as fuel for the royal fireplace, and quarrel between themselves over who gets the best seat in front of the resulting blaze? Surely this is not a responsible use of power. Rather, the King and Queen must encourage their kingdom to grow and prosper; they must try to produce more food, to plant trees for additional building material, to improve the lives of their subjects, and to live together justly in peace and love. They must work for the well-being of their domain.

Genesis 1:28 specifically describes how we are to rule the earth. After creating man and woman, God gave them their working orders: "Be fruitful and increase in number; fill the earth and subdue it. Rule over the fish of the sea and the birds of the air and over every living creature that moves on the ground." Although God gave this responsibility to human beings before the fall, he reaffirms this unique vocation throughout the Scriptures. As we carry out our responsibility to rule over God's creation, we must follow one simple command: we are to love God and to love our neighbor as ourselves (Matthew 22:37–40).

In fulfilling our responsibilities, we work to establish a world in which we are in complete harmony with God, our fellow creatures, and the natural world. The Bible calls this perfect order *shalom.* Our efforts to bring shalom involve us in three specific duties that can be met in part by reading literature: 1) we are to cultivate the potentials of God's world; 2) we are to enjoy a world of delight; 3) we are to work for a world of physical sustenance and justice.

Cultivating God's World

Adam and Eve's rule of Eden provides a helpful example for us. God's original creation was not immutable, not changeless perfection. The garden grew. Herbs and trees were to turn to seed, birds and fish were to multiply and fill the environment, human beings were both "to fill" and "to work and take care" of the world God created (Gen. 1:11–12, 22, 28; 2:15). In ruling Eden, Adam and Eve were to expand on the unrealized potentials that God had created in his world. They were not to conquer the garden; they were to cultivate it.

Similarly, we are to develop the multiple potentials inherent in creation. We are to produce science and technology, social and political structures, and works of visual art, music, and literature as part of our expansion of God's world. Calvin Seerveld, professor at the Institute for Christian Studies in Toronto, speaks strongly of the Christian's responsibility to develop the world: "Culture is not optional. . . . To fight cultural amplification of creation is to be disobedient to the will of the Lord revealed in the Scriptures" (24). Human beings have a responsibility to develop God's creation.

In producing works of literature, we obey God's command. Nicholas Barker, a poet and professor of literature, defines art (including the art of literature) as the "unfolding of previously unrealized potentialities in the aesthetic dimension of creation, or . . . the exercise on the part of artists of their God-ordained dominion over the aesthetic dimension of creation" (16). The way writers cultivate language and literary forms is a central part of their human vocation.

But writers also take raw materials from the world around them as they cultivate God's creation. They employ historical events, scientific facts, cultural beliefs, philosophical principles and very often spiritual experiences in their works. As we read, we encounter the many possible human reactions to life and explore the infinite options of God's world. Reading helps us to discover some of the incredible possibilities and inevitable limitations of life. God's command that we fill and cultivate the earth, then, can be accomplished in part through the writing and reading of literature.

As any gardener knows, though, cultivation goes beyond just adding more plants. Our duty is both to "fill" and to "subdue" the earth. Nicholas Wolterstorff explains the concept of subduing as involving the imposition of order: "Man is to continue God's work of bringing forth order, cosmos" (76).

A good cultivator will encourage growth by carefully ordering that growth. A cultivated garden has the weeds removed, the wild shoots pinched, and the unruly branches pruned. In Book IX of *Paradise Lost*, the seventeenth-century English poet John Milton imagines Adam and Eve's cultivation as involving this kind of ordering. The couple "prune, or prop, or bind" various plants during their daily labors. Eve reinforces heavy rose bushes with myrtle bands, while Adam trains the climbing ivy. Even as God imposed order by structuring the cosmos in creation, so Adam and Eve impose order in the expanding world.

Writing and reading continue these acts of ordering. Writers do not merely pour words or ideas out on a page in an unformed and chaotic manner; rather, they fashion their works carefully. Similarly, as we read and interpret, or use metaphors and stories, we act to structure and order life.

One of the consequences of the fall is the need for more cultivation. Because of sin, the creation's potential has often been warped during its development. Milton's rose bushes and ivy have grown out of control and become ugly parodies of themselves. Consequently, we now must reorder all aspects of creation to be pleasing to God. We must read and write as responsible Christians, pulling weeds and taming unruly growth. The last part of this book examines some of the ways to select and to evaluate what we read—to distinguish roses from ragweed.

Enjoying God's World

Milton's account of the Garden of Eden not only shows Adam and Eve engaged in their task of cultivation, but also vividly depicts their delight in God's creation. Book IV of *Paradise Lost* describes an idyllic scene as Adam and Eve eat their dinner:

> to their supper fruits they fell,
> Nectarine fruits which the compliant boughs
> Yielded them, sidelong as they sat recline
> On the soft downy bank damasked with flowers
> The savory pulp they chew, and in the rind
> Still as they thirsted scoop the brimming stream;
> Nor gentle purpose, nor endearing smiles
> Wanted, nor youthful dalliance, as beseems
> Fair couple linked in happy nuptial league,
> Alone as they. About them frisking played
> All beasts of th' earth, since wild, and of all chase
> In wood or wilderness, forest or den.

Sporting the lion ramped, and in his paw
Dandled the kid; bears, tigers, ounces, pards,
Gamboled before them; th' unwieldly elephant,
To make them mirth, used all his might, and wreathed
His lithe proboscis. (331–47)

Adam and Eve have worked enough to enjoy their leisure. Dining on
luscious fruits, they flirt with each other as the animals romp around
them, trying to make them laugh.

Milton's account is undeniably appealing; it is also biblically sound.
Genesis describes Eden as a garden, full of animal and plant life and
featuring numerous trees "pleasing to the eye and good for food"
(2:9). Some are useful trees, good to eat, providing nourishment. But
others are trees just to enjoy, delightful in their beauty. The world
that God gave humans at creation provided not only sustenance but
also delight. Although as a result of sin our capacity for enjoyment
is much diminished and often wrongly directed, delight is still an
important part of God's plan for us.

The psalmist celebrates how God's gifts give enjoyment:

He makes grass grow for the cattle,
    and plants for man to cultivate—
    bringing forth food from the earth:
wine that gladdens the heart of man,
    oil to make his face shine,
    and bread that sustains his heart. (Psalm 104:14–15)

The wine, oil, and bread nourish the body but also gladden the heart.
In my church we celebrate God's gifts every Sunday in our remem-
brance of his greatest gift, salvation. Just before we come forward to
share communion, the minister holds high a cup of wine and a loaf
of bread and joyfully proclaims, "The gifts of God for the people of
God!"

The celebration of the Eucharist reminds us of the reason we have
for our joy and delight: the reality of the resurrection. Jesus came to
earth to give us the means to recapture the ability to feel true joy.
After telling his disciples of his love for them and their need to obey

his commands, Jesus explains, "I have told you this so that my joy may be in you and that your joy may be complete" (John 15:11). God's creative and redemptive acts make delight possible.

Our delight in God's gifts should include, then, our delight in the literary activities of our fellow human beings. When God finished his wondrous work of creation, he surveyed all that he had made and pronounced it "very good." He stopped to appreciate and enjoy what he had made. In the same way, we appreciate the beautiful language and emotion of a poem, delight in an effective metaphor, feel awe at the dramatic effectiveness of a scene in a play, or acknowledge the skill with which a novelist portrays a character. In all these acts of enjoyment we act as God would have us act.

We often find it difficult to accept the validity of pure delight. The Roman poet Horace claimed that the purpose of literature was "to teach and to delight," but in thinking about literature, too often Christians are only interested in what it teaches or how it instructs. God ordained both delight and usefulness as part of his purposes for creation. We have no right to conclude that literature that primarily instructs us is somehow better in God's eyes than literature that primarily delights us.

In acknowledging the skill of an author or the beauty of a work of literature, we praise the great Creator of the heavens and the earth. Delight in a well-crafted work of literature is a response to God. Humans can develop the artistic potentials of language, metaphor, and narrative only because God created a world of potential beauty. When we say "this is good," delighting in the beauty of literature, we follow God's response to his own creative act.

Loving Our Neighbors

In addition to enjoying God's bounty, Christians should serve human needs. We must seek to build a world in which we acknowledge God and delight in his goodness, and in which people live together in love and justice. If we are to stand in right relationship with God, we must order his creation in such a way that we demonstrate our love to our neighbor.

What does the familiar concept of loving our neighbor as ourselves entail? The responsibility to love is a responsibility to take action. We must not just love passively in theory by having a loving attitude. Instead, as the parable of the Good Samaritan shows so forcefully, we must act purposefully to improve the spiritual, physical, and emotional conditions of others.

In Jesus's story about the final judgment in Matthew 25, the King praises the righteous for taking action: feeding the hungry, refreshing the thirsty, entertaining the stranger, clothing the naked, caring for the sick, and visiting the prisoners. Our attempts to bring about God's kingdom include these physical acts of love which are attempts to reorder the creation to serve our fellow human beings.

At least two things hinder us as we try to love our neighbor: ignorance and selfishness. Often, knowing little of other people's lives, we are content to remain in our own world. We never consider the handicapped man in the row next to us, the elderly woman in the local rest home, the struggling Christian behind the Iron Curtain, or the terrorized Central American villager. Our selfishness contributes to our ignorance because we often deliberately choose to see only our own little world. But our ignorance also contributes to our selfishness when we fail to see how we can love our neighbor, develop effective ways to help others, and bring about changes in corrupted systems.

Reading literature can help us to love others and to construct a world that demonstrates that love, because one of its functions is to increase our knowledge. Some poems, such as a Japanese haiku etching the fragile tension of a spiderweb, add to our understanding of beauty. Other kinds of poems provide more complex information. Milton's *Paradise Lost*, T. S. Eliot's *The Waste Land*, and Allen Ginsberg's *Howl* are in their own ways as skillfully crafted as a haiku, but they are also poetic comments on how to make sense of the confusions of life. In examining the way the text explores possibilities, we increase our understanding of God's world, ourselves, and our neighbors.

In the first place, reading a variety of works can expand our factual knowledge of other times, places, and people. If we explore a wide variety of literature, we will read about parts of the physical and historical world we might never visit in time and space. Such accounts can broaden our knowledge both of God's world and of how humans have chosen to live in that world.

While we may never travel to Argentina, an Argentinian novel may allow us to visualize its wide treeless pampas, to learn about its political and social structures, and to understand the differing attitudes of the Argentinian general and the Argentinian peasant. We will never live in medieval England, but the poetry of Geoffrey Chaucer tells us about medieval customs, thought, and life. We may not live in an inner-city housing development, but a poem about life in the ghetto may bring home to us the sights, smells, and voices of American poverty. The more we know of others, the better our chance to understand their situation and to hear their concerns.

Paradoxically, we can understand others better when we begin to see ourselves more clearly, recognizing our failings and humanity. Self-awareness may come to us in a flash of recognition, as we see a parallel between ourselves and a character, emotion, or idea. Such sudden insight may illuminate what we have unconsciously hidden from ourselves. Jane Austen's *Pride and Prejudice* works this way for me; as I read about the experiences of Elizabeth Bennet, I uncover my own pride and tendency toward prejudice. Before I can love others, I must understand these faults of my own. While the self-knowledge prompted by a text can lead to self-loathing, as Christians we live in a world where forgiveness is possible, and where recognizing our inadequacies can prepare us to love others.

When we find ourselves in the texts that we read, we begin to understand some of the many similarities we have with our neighbors. The "other" is not completely other, as Jesus indicates by choosing to talk about our responsibility to other people in terms of loving our "neighbor." People often share the same problems, the same longings, the same fears. When we read about Sammy, the grocery clerk who defends the right of three girls to shop in their bikinis in John

Updike's "A & P," we understand his actions in light of our own appreciation of beauty and inept attempts to pursue justice. We see ourselves in Sammy's awkward behavior, and so begin to understand how the "other" can actually be our neighbor.

Similarities between ourselves and texts help us to love our neighbor, but points of difference can have the same effect. Have you ever had a discussion with someone who took a completely different approach to an issue than you did? Such a discussion can show you another way of thinking about a topic (breaking through self-centeredness) but can also strengthen your own understanding of and faith in your position (giving self-awareness).

In a similar way, encountering new ideas in a text may allow you to understand your neighbor but also may allow you to understand yourself more clearly in juxtaposition. Literature professor Henry Zylstra explains the way this process works:

There is a real sense in which it [literature] enables us by vicarious experience in our life to bring to bear on being Christian, myriads of lives not our own. I suppose that the way the philosophers would say it is this, that by universalizing ourselves in the significant experience of others there is more of us that is Christian, that can be Christian, than there was before. There is more of you, after reading Hardy, to be Christian with than there was before you read him, and there is also more conviction that you want to be it. (67)

In reading *Tess of the D'Urbervilles*, we find the English novelist Thomas Hardy exploring some of the possibilities of life. We may never have considered seriously the despair one can feel at the apparently random events of life or how easily Christian charity may fail when confronted with sexual immorality. By making us think about these things, reading Hardy may give us new attitudes or opinions. After we read Hardy, our Christianity may include a heightened sensitivity and sympathy.

Another way we can advance toward love is to understand ourselves and our neighbors in relation to the culture and society in which we live. The historian George Marsden explains that we need "a perspective that will help destroy our self-made, self-centered worlds. With an historical perspective it will become much more difficult to believe that the world really revolves around ourselves or that the values and ideals of our culture and our era are the best there have ever been" (33).

When we read, we hear the values and ideals of other cultures. The poetry of Anne Bradstreet tells us how the American Puritans struggled to adjust to the hardships of the new world and tried to reconcile physical and spiritual events; Pope expresses eighteenth-century ideas about decorum and order; Dickens depicts how the Victorians viewed and treated children; Hemingway voices the aimlessness and despair felt by many Americans after World War I. As we listen to and think about these ideas, we understand our own values better, and we may even refine or adjust our ideas based on our expanded vision.

Our reading of texts thus leads us to what critic Robert Scholes terms "extratextual concerns." As we read, we see Bradstreet's poems or Dickens' novels "not simply as styles or modes of production in an isolated realm of 'art,' but as world views with social consequences" (38). We critique Pope's rationalism or Hemingway's naturalism and seek to understand how such attitudes affect the way one lives. We try to find the best way to carry out our lives in accordance with God's directives.

Besides learning about the values of other societies, we can also recognize the limits of our own twentieth-century American perspective when we understand the extent to which our ideas have been constructed by culture and society. When we read works from the past and examine the social and historical conditions that influenced their formation, we learn how meaning and expression are to a certain extent limited by history. Such an awareness is necessary in order for us to evaluate our own situation and attempt to break free of those constraints which keep us from serving God and loving our neighbor.

Here's a rather simple example of this complex idea: Think of a story about war. Imagine the instruments of destruction. You may have seen a sophisticated jet fighter, a mushroom-shaped cloud, unerring MX missiles, or spider-like helicopters hovering over a tropical jungle. These images of war are post-nuclear, post-Vietnam images, possible only in the 1980s. When Sir Thomas Malory wrote *Morte D'arthur* in the 1470s, he characterized the ultimate war with very different images:

> And never since was there never seen a more dolefuller battle in no Christian land, for there was but rushing and riding, foining and striking; and many a grim word was there spoken of either to other, and many a deadly stroke. . . .
>
> And thus they fought all the long day, and never stinted till the noble knights were laid to the cold earth. And ever they fought still till it was near night, and by then was there an hundred thousand laid dead upon the down.

As we try to understand the reality and meaning of war, we employ images and narratives. But these images and narratives arise out of our cultural situation, and so our understanding of war is influenced by our historical situation.

If we see that our concepts of war are to a certain extent (although not completely) a product of our culture, we can gain insight into the stories into which we were born and that influence us. Such insight can allow us to reevaluate the appropriateness of these stories and their values.

Remember the discussion of Benjamin Franklin's *Autobiography* in chapter 3? We examined some of the cultural and social influences that went into its composition (eighteenth-century rationalism, Franklin's religious upbringing) and then looked at how this story has become an influential American myth. In reading Franklin's book, we may learn that some of our own ideas about hard work and success come more from this cultural figure than from our Christian principles. My students are often surprised to discover that certain sayings they had always thought to be from Proverbs were actually from Franklin's *Poor Richard's Almanac*. Rather than simply accepting the success story as one we should all copy, we see its origins and reconsider its validity.

In conclusion, reading literature broadens our vision as we increase our knowledge of ourselves, others, culture, and history. We enlarge our perspective not in order to condemn others or to point out their many errors, but in order to explore God's world more thoroughly, to understand our neighbors better, and to work for shalom more effectively. Knowledge and understanding can result in analysis and action as we reform the distortions in our own attitudes and in social, economic, political, and religious systems.

Our responsibilities to God, to the cultivation and enhancement of his creation, and to the love and care of human beings give focus to our lives. Our reading of literature is part of the way we fulfill these responsibilities and carry out our unique vocation.

Chapter 5

KEEPING LITERATURE IN PERSPECTIVE

Literature has its limits, and we need to keep its value in perspective. Consider two apparently paradoxical facts. First, very few people actually read the works that we study in literature courses; such reading is an activity confined to those who are educated and have leisure time. Most of the people in the world—the millions of Chinese peasants, the starving Ethiopians, the impoverished Indians of South America—do not read literary texts. For these people, physical survival is a more important issue than literature. Our ability to create, interpret, and enjoy literature is a special privilege.

On the other hand, even though reading Dante, Shakespeare, and Faulkner is a privileged activity, all people in all circumstances employ metaphor and narrative, attempt to make sense out of their lives, and use words to create artistic works. While some cultures may not have written literature, all cultures produce works of art that depend on the concepts of meaning and interpretation.

During the nineteenth century, enslaved black Americans seldom knew how to read or write, but they nonetheless composed songs, told folktales to their children, and brought meaning to their lives by viewing their experience metaphorically as Israel's captivity in Egypt. Their literature was oral. Cultures without a written language or without much leisure time nonetheless produce epics, ballads, folktales, songs, proverbs, and oral histories. These works are passed on by memory rather than by writing. The production and consumption of some form of literature is a universal phenomenon.

Though all people have some kind of literature, the Western world has made literature into an institution, a type of big business. We have elaborate systems that control the production and consumption of literature. This gigantic institutionalization of the process of reading includes publishing firms, book stores, bestseller lists, the celebrity status of the latest author to appear on Johnny Carson, the deluge of coffee-table books in stores at Christmas, departments of English in high schools and colleges, graduate schools, academic journals, and tenure systems. Until recently, works of literature standing outside of this institution were often overlooked.

In understanding the value of literature and the many important ways that it can make a difference in our lives, we should keep in mind both the universality of literature (everyone has some kind of literature) and the special place that certain kinds of literature have in Western society.

A State of Crisis?

Ever since the nineteenth century, institutionalized literature has been increasingly on the defensive, as the introduction to this book has shown. Literature has long had its critics and its crusaders, but the debate has become more intense, strident, and impassioned during the last decade. The claims made on all sides of the debate are serious, so serious that many people believe that the study of literature is in a state of crisis.

Much of this controversy has arisen precisely because of the way that the Romantics glorified literature. If the value of literary texts lies solely in the imaginary worlds they create, then it may be valid to complain that reading literature is a waste of time and will not help one find a job. In part because of these complaints, many colleges began dropping literature and humanities requirements in the 1970s. In 1984, according to the National Endowment for the Humanities, a student could graduate from seventy-two percent of all American colleges and universities without having studied American literature or history (Bennett, 1–2).

Weakened by the lack of student interest, the study of literature is also under attack by some of its own practitioners—literary scholars and critics. Moving away from the Romantic idea of literature, several new critical theories suggest that literature is merely a big language game that readers play by interpreting stories to fit their own personalities and needs. Literature is an object that provides a kind of diversion. Roland Barthes, a French philosopher and literary critic, describes reading in sexual terms and talks about "the pleasure of the text" (58). For many contemporary critics, this pleasure emerges from their own ability to discover conflicting or multiple interpretations. Denis Donoghue calls such critics "graphireaders" and explains,

When you watch Marcel Marceau, you know that his moving fingers are his fingers but you also know that they are a butterfly. . . . Graphireaders are not interested in the butterfly: they want to play with the possibilities disclosed in a relation between their minds and Marceau's moving fingers; they want to produce new events from their minds and his fingers, and they despise as banal the pleasure of recognizing a butterfly issuing from an actor's digits. (152)

In ignoring the butterfly, these critics often also ignore the power of literature to affect the real world.

Readers who are only interested in the pleasure they can gain from playing with the text clearly are hedonistic, but we should be careful not to err too far in the other direction and claim too much for the power of literature. One of the most common ways to defend literature is to argue that great works of literature have a kind of redemptive power, that if everyone would just read more literature, the world would be a better place. Christians must reject this perspective also.

During a time of turmoil, bewildered people often turn to literature as a way to solve some of society's problems. The argument for the redemptive power of literature became especially urgent in the nineteenth century, when many began to reject historical Christianity and sought a new set of moral rules. Writing in 1880, the British poet and critic Matthew Arnold stated:

The future of poetry is immense, because in poetry, where it is worthy of its high destinies, our race, as time goes on, will find an ever surer and surer stay. There is not a creed which is not shaken, not an accredited dogma which is not shown to be questionable, not a received tradition which does not threaten to dissolve. . . . More and more mankind will discover that we have to turn to poetry to interpret life for us, to console us, to sustain us. Without poetry, our science will appear incomplete; and most of what now passes with us for religion and philosophy will be replaced by poetry.

Arnold turned to literature for salvation at a time when a Christian cultural consensus was collapsing under the weight of new arguments in theology, philosophy, and science.

We face similar turmoil in today's society. In a world of Wall Street corruption, irrational terrorists, and the threat of nuclear annihilation, some scholars argue that literature can offer solutions, that literature is valuable because it forms better people. As we read great works of literature, individually we become more humane people and collectively we become a more humane society.

Exactly how does literature make us more humane? If we think about it as the imaginative creation of a special world, as Northrop Frye does, we see that in such a world the disorder of life can be left behind. Literature has consoling, almost therapeutic powers. But because Frye makes such a distinction between "home" and "environment," this power can only affect a person's feelings and can never be transformed into action to change the social or political realities of the world.

A second argument for literature's humanizing power suggests that when readers encounter important issues in literature, they become more concerned with moral values. Because literature often deals with important ethical issues—such as "What is justice?" "How can we best love others?" "What are the mutual responsibilities of parents and children?"—some literary critics believe that people develop life-affirming values when exposed to literature that asks such questions.

This point of view certainly has some merit. However, even if a person gains a new sensitivity to moral issues by reading, his or her actions may not necessarily change. We can find many examples that disprove the theory that reading literature produces ethical people. Terry Eagleton, a leading Marxist critic, points to the Nazi commandant at Auschwitz, who relaxed after a day of supervising massive human destruction by reading Goethe.

Another literary scholar, June Goodfield, writes,

Let us ask ourselves if the Shakespearean plays, with their almost God-like insight into the way that people behave, made people understand more, act better, or feel nicer—more humane. . . . The people who went to the Globe Theatre and saw those marvelous dramas, with their rich poetry and their human understanding, would at the same place, in the same afternoon, watch a monkey tied to the back of a horse being chased by dogs who slowly bit it to death. I think it unfair and unwise to create a myth of the therapeutic power of the humanities. (3)

Reading great works of literature does not necessarily make us more loving. Some defenders of literature claim too much for its redeeming power.

Between Two Extremes

A Christian perspective on reading lies between the extremes of hedonism and redemption. Books are neither objects of pure pleasure or instruments of unlimited power. Instead, they are one way in which humans have developed the potentials of God's world. Literary works can give pleasure and exercise power only because they are part of the world that God structured, and readers have the freedom to use what is expressed in literature for good or for evil.

The beauty of a text, as a Christian understands it, honors God. Our delight in a well-constructed work should be a form of praise to God for granting us the ability to read and write. A literary work belongs to God's created world; it is not an independent cosmos created only for pleasure. As part of God's world, works of literature are not mere language games but products of human beings who are deeply enmeshed in specific historical situations.

On the question of the saving power of literature, Christians acknowledge that the only way to become better people is through Christ's redeeming grace. We can love our neighbor only because Christ first loved us. Literature will never replace religion, as Matthew Arnold hoped, for it is not powerful enough or truthful enough to change people on its own. However, reading literature can help us follow God's commands. Prompted by our desire to serve God, we attempt to cultivate his creation in a pleasing and life-sustaining fashion. We do so by using every possible resource, including the rich resources of reading. Only the working of the Spirit can transform an understanding of literature's moral issues into action.

Literature exposes us to many important ideas and moral concerns; it teaches us our cultural heritage and helps to preserve the collective ideals of our society. Literature contains worthy examples and vivid warnings of errors. However, many readers never move from discovering these truths to implementing them in action.

Finally, by understanding that literature is one of the ways that human beings cultivate the potentials of God's creation, we can see literature's universal nature. The fact that all people in all societies have some type of literature shows that God created us to be metaphor makers and story tellers. Although we may choose to pay special attention to those works of literature that are part of our Western institution of literature, we should also acknowledge that works outside the institution have value and are important.

Reading literature is thus an important part of our participation in the world. It does much more than give us hedonistic pleasure or therapeutic escape from our dingy world. While it does not have the power to force us to become more humane, the act of reading can make a great difference in our lives. Reading literature carefully can be one way that we act as responsible Christians to serve our Lord and delight in his gifts.

PART 2

What Happens When We Read?

Chapter 6

HOW SHOULD WE READ?

Reading can be a frightening activity. It can be terrifying to sit down, without a clue, to read a strange and difficult piece of literature. After all, it is the rare person who can read through Milton's *Paradise Lost* or Chaucer's *Canterbury Tales* unassisted at the age of nineteen. For most of us, the first reading of a classic is more likely to be a matter of guesswork and confusion than of confident assessment and ease. When we are told to read one of the classics, it is only natural to wonder, *"How* am I supposed to read this thing?"

When we ask such a question, we may well be looking for a very specific answer. In the back of our minds may lurk the belief that someone can tell us how to read Dostoevsky's novel *The Brothers Karamazov,* in the same way that good instructions would show us how to fill out IRS Form 1040, how to assemble a carburetor, or how to repair a crack in a plaster wall. After all, we might think, learning how to do something is more a matter of taking things apart and putting them back together than anything else; if there can be a recipe for baking a cake, why can't there be one for reading a novel?

But is this process of applying a clear-cut method to a text the correct way to go about reading a book? Is this what we actually do when we read a poem, play, or novel? Do we sit down, pull our analytical tools out of our intellectual bags, and proceed to operate upon the work? We can develop sophisticated techniques for analyzing works of literature, but what if literature is not something to be figured out in the same way as a cookbook or car repair manual? What if the very act of putting a work of literature at arm's length for analysis robs it of its power to address us with authority?

This chapter will consider questions such as these. In addition, it will examine the historical frame of reference for what has become a common way of thinking about the question, "How should I read this book?" The answer may not be as simple as we have believed it to be.

The Claim of a Work of Art Upon Us

In courses in the classics of Western literature—on Christian college campuses and at public universities alike—St. Augustine's *Confessions* is often taught as a work of great literature. It is acknowledged to be one of the finest autobiographies ever written, and many who do not share Augustine's Christian beliefs consider the *Confessions* a work of genuine merit. But regardless of what the reader of Augustine believes about Christianity, he or she has to ask the question, "*How* is this book to be read?" As a work of probing self-analysis, should the *Confessions* be read primarily as a book that has deep psychological significance? Or in reading it, should we concentrate on what it reveals to us about the economic or social history of the decaying Roman empire of the fourth century? Or—and this is the question we are most likely to ask in a literature class—should we read it as a work of literary art, with our efforts geared to the discovery of the symbolic richness of its language and the intricate patterns of its form?

Interestingly enough, Augustine provides within the *Confessions* an excellent example of the problems raised by the question, "*How* should I read this book?" The example comes from what is perhaps the key scene in the entire work, Augustine's description of his conversion. Because of its importance, the passage is worth quoting at some length:

I flung myself down on the ground somehow under a fig tree and gave free rein to my tears; they streamed and flooded from my eyes, an *acceptable sacrifice to Thee*. And I kept saying to you, not perhaps in these words, but with this sense: "*And Thou, Oh Lord, how long? How long, Lord; wilt Thou be angry forever? Remember not our former iniquities. . . .*"

Suddenly a voice reaches my ears from a nearby house. It is the voice of a boy or a girl (I don't know which) and in a kind of singsong the words are constantly repeated: "Take it and read it. Take it and read it." . . . I checked the force of my tears and rose to my feet, being quite certain that I must interpret this as a divine command to me to open [the Scriptures] and read the first passage which I should come upon. For I had heard this about Anthony: he had happened to come in when the Gospel was being read, and as though the words were spoken directly to himself, had received the admonition: *Go, sell all that thou hast, and give to the poor, and thou shalt have treasure in heaven, and come and follow me.* And by such an oracle he had been immediately converted to you.

So I went eagerly back to the place where Alypius [Augustine's friend] had been sitting, since it was there that I had left the book of the Apostle when I rose to my feet. I snatched up the book, opened it, and read in silence the passage upon which my eyes first fell: *Not in rioting and drunkenness, not in chambering and wantonness, not in strife and envying: but put ye on the Lord Jesus Christ, and make not provision for the flesh in concupiscence.* I had no wish to read further; there was no need to. For immediately I had reached the end of this sentence it was as though my heart was filled with a light of confidence and all the shadows of my doubt were swept away. (182–83)

Augustine's response to the phrase chanted by those children seems irrational by any modern standard. Having come to a point of spiritual agony in his restless and dissolute life, Augustine hears this children's phrase and takes it as a command to go and read the Scriptures. He opens a copy and reads the first verse that comes before his eyes. And in reading it, he believes he hears the specific will of God commanding him to repent. For the rest of his life, the saint will look back to this experience as the turning point of his life.

Though Augustine was a brilliant interpreter of culture and a very careful reader of texts, his method of reading at this extraordinary moment is loose and unmethodical. He believes that a randomly chosen passage of scripture represents the command of the Lord. Because there is nothing precise or detached in Augustine's handling of the passage that comes to him unexpectedly, some modern readers might argue that there is something inherently suspicious about the way he reads this text. In order to understand the passage properly, Augustine would have to analyze it objectively. Specifically, as a literary critic, he would consider its qualities as a work of art. He might look for rhythmic patterns or clusters of images; he might try to place this brief passage in a larger framework of symbols or stories. In any case, a proper course of action, according to this view of reading, would involve setting the text aside for objective analysis. That is *how one ought to read*, it might be argued.

In fact, such a detached approach to the Bible is precisely what the editors of *The Literary Guide to the Bible* advocate. In their introduction, Robert Alter and Frank Kermode acknowledge that the Bible may be read as a book reporting the action of God in human history, or as a source of truth and correct values. But the editors believe that those who read the Bible in this way represent a minority in modern secular culture. So, instead of trying to revive a sense of the Bible as a sacred text, the editors offer "a new view of the Bible as a work of great literary force and authority" (2). They even claim that "literary analysis must come first" before all other uses of the Bible. Without prior literary analysis, the other ways of using the Bible will remain hopelessly misguided, for unless we have a sound understanding of how the text fits together as a literary work, "it will not be of much value in other respects"(2).

The fact that Alter and Kermode's approach does not seem disturbing, even to some Christian readers, is a sign of how thoroughly our culture has accepted the idea of written texts as art objects. It is also a sign of the gulf that separates the modern world from a man like Augustine. Although he had a critical intellect and carefully scrutinized the countless texts he read by Christian and pagan contemporaries and by great authors of the Greek, Roman, and Christian past, Augustine also had a keen understanding of the power of written works to command our attention and demand our allegiance. That did not mean, of course, for Augustine or other Christians of the ancient world, that one accepted on principle the claims of any powerful text. With the exception of the Scriptures, which they would have considered to have a special authority, such thinkers would have held that the claims made by works had to be scrutinized and challenged but could not be ignored.

To see possible consequences of the developments that have separated us from the world of Augustine, let us look briefly at another passage. This one is from the New Testament:

> We are hard pressed on every side, but not crushed; perplexed, but not in despair; persecuted, but not abandoned; struck down, but not destroyed. We always carry around in our body the death of Jesus, so that the life of Jesus may also be revealed in our body. For we who are alive are always being given over to death for Jesus' sake, so that his life may be revealed in our mortal body. (2 Corinthians 4:8–11)

The Apostle Paul's prose is packed with vivid metaphors and striking parallel constructions. Rich in image patterns and exciting rhythms, this passage is poetry indeed.

But if we concentrate exclusively on the "poetry" of this passage, what happens? Quite simply, it loses its power to address us with authority. When we are about the business of exploring its poetic richness, it is hard for us to hear any claim the passage might be seeking to make upon us. When you are dissecting an alligator or examining the disassembled parts of a "dead" warhead, you don't worry much about the damage the thing in question might do to you. For when you have it under analysis, it is at your mercy, under your control.

A contemporary German thinker, Hans-Georg Gadamer, has written at length about what happens when we approach a work of literature, or any work of art, in this detached manner. He speaks of the alienation this approach can bring on. The aesthetic attitude "distinguishes the aesthetic quality of a work from all elements of content which induce us to take up an attitude towards it, moral or religious" (77). In the "aesthetic" approach, the critic is involved exclusively in the contemplation of the work of art, and questions of truth and significance are set to one side. When we analyze a work of poetry or fiction in this manner, we examine it for qualities that we can admire because of their beauty or orderliness. We attend not so much to *what* is said through the work of literature, but to the *way* it is said.

According to Gadamer and others, this aesthetic distancing, which places the question of truth at arm's length, is a recent development in the history of thought about literature and the other arts. Though Homer, Augustine, and Dante are taught in literature classes, it would have been unthinkable for these authors to have considered their writings primarily as works of "literary art." Of course, each demonstrated a superb creative ability in his use of language. But though each was sensitive to the power and beauty of words, his central concern was to have his works make a claim upon those who heard or read them. In a fundamental sense, these authors would have thought of their works as proclamations of truths to be heard rather than as beautiful depictions of feelings to be viewed with detachment.

This discussion of Augustine, St. Paul, and others should not in any way be taken as an argument in favor of refusing to apply methods of analysis to works of literature. The close reading of poems, plays, and works of fiction plays a vital part in the study of literature. To understand fully a lyric poem by William Wordsworth or George Herbert, a reader will want to know how to scan the metrical patterns of the poem and how to detect the play of metaphor and the allusions to the Bible and to history. In a similar way, to comprehend the importance of a novel by Charlotte Brontë or F. Scott Fitzgerald, a reader will need to be sensitive to rhythmic developments in the prose style and alert to archetypal images and patterns of story-telling. Close analysis may enrich our understanding of a work of literature, and later chapters of this book will discuss in detail ways of analyzing literary texts.

It is important, however, to keep in mind the role of such analysis. Though it can help to deepen our understanding of what we read, it cannot take the place of the initial act of comprehension that happens when we read a book. If we begin our reading of any work by putting it at a safe, analytical distance from us, we run the risk of rendering that work powerless to speak to us. And when books stop speaking to us—or when other people and events no longer speak to us—we are in danger of forgetting how to learn.

How Did We Get to This Point?

To a significant extent, our present beliefs about literature developed in the eighteenth and early nineteenth centuries. The literary historian M. H. Abrams has explored the origins of what he terms the "modern theory of 'art-as-such'," which he sees as a common theme in modern thinking about literature. According to this view, works of art are clearly distinguished from "all other human products," because of the qualities inherent in them or the responses they provoke. They exist to be contemplated in a disinterested fashion, for their own sake, and not because they necessarily point to a world or truth outside themselves. "To many of us, such assertions also seem to be patent truths," says Abrams, "confirmed by our ordinary experience of works of art. The historical facts, however, should give us pause." Though we may believe that our present conception of art is a view that has been held since the beginning of recorded time, history shows that this is clearly not the case (Abrams, "Kant," 75–76).

To understand some of the difficulties involved in this modern view of "art-as-such," think of the experience of gazing at pictures on the wall of an art museum. I can recall my first visit to the Art Institute of Chicago when I was a sophomore in college. An eccentric but lively professor brought our class to the museum to explore its treasures. He did an excellent job of explaining several paintings and describing the general shape of the Art Institute's collections. He was especially careful to introduce us to the strict etiquette of museums. First, you are to keep very quiet, he told us. When gazing at a painting, you must stand behind the rope, with hands folded behind your back; and if you gesture at a painting, you must do so with your palm and your entire hand extended, he told us. All of us in the class felt there was something sacred about the whole process.

Yet I remember most distinctly the strange experience of going off on my own in the museum to examine works I had never heard of by artists whose names were foreign to me. I had learned the appropriate gestures of museum observation, but I had no idea what I was supposed to find in the works displayed from different cultures in different centuries. As I gazed attentively at the paintings, I had little context in which to judge them and little idea of what questions I should be asking. The beautiful colors and forms impressed me, but I was glad for the hushed reverence of the place, because in silence I was able to hide my utter confusion.

To understand why a person might feel bewildered in a situation like this, think of a painting from medieval Europe or a piece of sculpture from ancient Greece that you might see in such a museum. Was it created to hang on those walls or stand in that space? In all likelihood, the painting was created as an image to aid in worship, and the sculpture probably stood in the center of a public place. The person who saw that painting or sculpture in its original setting understood its meaning by recognizing its place in the life of his or her church or community.

Thus it is that the objects we now contemplate in museums were first created for very different uses than we now make of them. It is unlikely that before 1750 anyone would have thought of a work of art as an object to be contemplated as an end in itself, or that anyone would have distinguished "aesthetic" responses from other valid responses to poems, plays, or stories.

We in the West began to think of art in a "museum" sense in the eighteenth century. Surprisingly enough, one of the strongest influences on the development of the "art-as-such" view was the debate at that time about the nature of ethics, or what it was that made for right human action. One influential thinker, the Earl of Shaftesbury, argued against the cynical views of human behavior in his day. He claimed that a person with a true love of God should not think of rewards and punishments, but should worship God for his own sake. Truly ethical behavior for Shaftesbury was a matter of "loving" the "view or contemplation" of virtue; to love God was to adore him for what he was regardless of what he might do for or against you.

At first glance, such dated discussions about ethics might seem irrelevant, for how can old comments about the nature of virtue be important for understanding literature? The answer is in the doctrine of *disinterestedness* as Shaftesbury espoused it. Disinterested action is behavior "free from selfish motive or interest," he argued, and a person should love God because it is right to do so, regardless of the consequences.

The German philosopher Immanuel Kant applied Shaftesbury's emphasis on ethical disinterestedness to the arts. Kant claimed that selfishness taints all actions, with the exception of the appreciation of art. He held that we can judge works of art "by means of a delight or aversion *apart from any interest.* The object of such a delight is called *beautiful"* (292). But even as he celebrated the artistic experience, he remained clear about its limits. Stressing the "disinterested" nature of the aesthetic experience, Kant described it as the "feeling of purposiveness without the idea of purpose." Kant held that in creating art we create alternate worlds in which to discover the purpose and order missing from our "real" world. But we should never forget, Kant claimed, that such worlds are the products of our imaginations rather than accurate images of reality.

Out of such thinking grew the widespread modern distinction between the "fine" and "useful" arts. In the "useful arts" we use art as a tool to assist us in our actions. We sing hymns to God, create images of the Virgin Mary to instill devotion in believers, or make attractive objects to hold and serve our daily food. In contrast, "the fine arts" have no purpose beyond themselves. Like God or the Good, the products of the fine arts are to be contemplated and admired in themselves and not as means to another end. While human beings study nature with the goal of mastering and using it, they may appreciate art with no end in sight but that of unselfish delight.

In modern discussions of literature and the other arts, Kant's ideas often seem to be accepted as matters of timeless common sense, even though they originated in a specific period in the cultural history of the West. To the Christian seeking to understand literature it is interesting to note that modern ideas about art arose as the cultural influence of Christianity began to decline. During the Enlightenment and Romantic periods, many of the now standard ideas about art were developed as means of dealing with the decline of orthodox faith.

As the earlier chapter on the nature of stories described, recent scholarship on the Romantic period has emphasized that the movement attempted to salvage the shell of Judeo-Christian values after orthodox belief had come under attack. The Romantics sought to maintain an aura of Christian belief by transferring to the *self* qualities formerly ascribed to God in Christian theism. M. H. Abrams says that romantic writers sought

> to save traditional concepts, schemes, and values which had been based on the relation of the Creator to his creature and creation, but to reformulate them within the prevailing two-term system of subject and object, ego and non-ego, the human mind or consciousness and its transactions with nature. (*Natural*, 13)

When eighteenth-century thoughts on disinterestedness were married to romantic ideas about the powers of the imagination, a potent understanding of literature was born. According to this view, the imaginative self, in its interaction with history and nature, takes on the powers of God. In 1817, the English poet and critic Samuel Taylor Coleridge wrote of the imagination that "it dissolves, diffuses, dissipates, in order to re-create; . . . it struggles to idealize and to unify. It is essentially vital, even as all objects (*as* objects) are essentially fixed and dead." According to Coleridge and many others after him, the imagination creates a lively alternate world, one in which we can indulge our desires without fear of harming others through our selfish actions.

By comparing the life-giving power of art to the deadly processes of nature, Emily Dickinson celebrates the poet's ability to create permanence and give delight:

Essential Oils—are wrung—
The Attar from the Rose
Be not expressed by Suns—alone—
It is the gift of Screws—

The General Rose—decay—
But this—in Lady's Drawer
Make Summer—When the Lady lie
In Ceaseless Rosemary

"Essential oils" are the perfumes produced by pressing the oil from a flower. More than the healthy vitality of the sun is required for their production, for it is "the gift of Screws" which wrings the lasting essence from the flower. In like manner, suffering presses upon the life of the poet and wrings from her a stunning object of lasting beauty. Though all natural things die ("The General Rose—decay—"), some special things endure ("But this—in Lady's Drawer / Make Summer—When the Lady lie / In Ceaseless Rosemary"). Whether "this—in Lady's Drawer" is a perfume or a poem, what matters is that the object which lasts is the one squeezed from life through a painful process. It alone has permanence, while other things pass away.

Dickinson's poem illustrates the way in which the modern aesthetic temperament searches for an innocent and enduring power in art. This view holds that art can give us the satisfactions formerly provided by religion and that it can provide such satisfaction without requiring particular intellectual or moral commitments from us. To find comfort in the form or beauty of a work of art, this view argues, may well be more important than responding to its claims about the truth.

How Then Should We Read?

Thus, under the influence of specific modern claims about literature, a number of critics have argued that a correct reading of literature must hold in abeyance the question of truth. Indeed, it is often said that the special beauty of art lies is its refusal to make claims about the truth. For example, in "The Figure a Poem Makes," Robert Frost wrote that a good poem "ends in a clarification of life—not necessarily a great clarification, such as sects and cults are founded on, but in a momentary stay against confusion." Poetry does not resolve questions of good and evil or truth and falsehood; unlike religion ("sects and cults"), it offers neither answers nor guidelines. Instead, it seeks only to present life's ambiguities in ways that are pleasant and surprising.

This is a questionable approach to literature, however, for anyone who believes that the making and appreciation of literature are forms of human action. Since our actions are founded upon our assumptions about what is right and true, questions of truth and ethics make a difference in our thinking about literature. Whenever we write a poem or watch a play, whenever we read a novel or describe an event we have witnessed, we are staking out a claim to truth. As both feminist and hermeneutical theory have pointed out repeatedly in recent years, those who write and those who read literature are always engaged in struggles over questions of truth and values. Whether we are aware of it or not, the poet and storyteller seek to make claims upon us.

When we read a work of literature, we respond to the claims being made upon us. We may like what we hear in the work, we may be confused by it, or we may find it offensive, but at a deep level we respond to *what* is said in what we read rather than to *how* it is said. This does not at all mean that *how* something is said is irrelevant. We cannot separate the language we use from the truths we wish to convey, so there can be no question of separating form from content. It is hard to study properly what is said if one remains ignorant of the way that it is said.

Form and content are inextricable. Any reading of any work of literature must attend to all that is said. This means that the answer to the question, "How am I supposed to read this book?" can never be a simple one. It cannot be simple, any more than the answers to questions such as "How am I to love my neighbor?" or "How am I to understand my parents' actions?" There are methods we can use in studying poems and stories, and they are discussed at length in later chapters of this book. But these methods can never take the place of the struggle we go through whenever we attempt to understand what has been said to us. There is no formula that we can "plug in" to solve the problem of reading a work of literature.

We learn to read in the same way that we learn to trust, to love, to command, and to obey. We learn through experience, through triumph and struggle; we learn to read well by doing a lot of reading, by reflecting upon our experiences, and by entering into conversation with others about what we have read. There are tools that can be of help in the work of interpreting, but nothing can take the place of practice in the craft. It takes time and genuine effort to learn how to read well. In an age in which we tout the virtues of "the one-minute manager" and crave both fast-food meals and quick weight-loss diets, patience and perseverance may seem unsatisfying as answers to the question, "how should I read this book?" But the wise person realizes that there are no shortcuts to learning how to read with wisdom, discernment, and appreciation.

Chapter 7

WHAT HAPPENS WHEN WE READ?

It is eleven o'clock on a Tuesday night; you've just picked up a can of soda and a bag of potato chips. Back at your room, you arrange your chair in just the right manner under your favorite light, pull your copy of Milton's *Paradise Lost* from the shelf, and sit down. To read.

To read. What happens as you read this poem by a famous seventeenth-century Englishman? How can you understand what Milton meant to say when he composed this work more than three hundred years ago? How can an ordinary reader discover anything new in *Paradise Lost?* After all, highly educated women and men have pored over the poem for centuries and have come up with very different things to say about it. In fact, many of the things that have been written about *Paradise Lost* are plainly contradictory. One authority says that the hero of this epic poem is Jesus; another claims that Adam and Eve are the central figures of the work; while still another critic and his followers argue that Satan, paradoxically enough, is the true hero of this Christian epic.

Faced with these contradictions, you might throw up your hands and say, "If these experts disagree, how can I hope to say anything meaningful about this poem?" Or you might respond with a bit of sarcasm, "Did the author intend *everything* we have said about this book?" And no matter what your questions are, you might wonder how you can have anything meaningful to add to what has already been said about this classic.

If issues of this kind trouble us as we sit down to read a difficult piece of literature, it may be that we have misunderstood the nature of the reading process by judging it naively according to the standards of science. To see what this means, think of what you did when you dissected a frog in eighth-grade science class or took a poll of your history class in the eleventh grade. You were not supposed to allow preconceptions about frogs to determine what you were going to see when you cut open your specimen; nor were you supposed to draw conclusions about the views of your fellow students before you conducted your interviews. In both cases, you wanted to approach your project with a open mind, as free as possible from the influence of groundless assumptions. You may have feared that if you failed to see things clearly, by letting your biases color your observations, then what you learned would not count as knowledge by scientific standards.

Many modern defenders of literature have concluded that the procedures of the scientist should also be those of the critic of literature. To that end, in this century many schools of criticism have attempted to develop rigorous, "scientific" approaches to literature. Though they may differ in a number of details, these critical approaches share a conviction that proper reading requires the setting aside of our biases. The diligent reader is to approach a poem or short story in the same way that we suppose the geologist begins the study of a collection of rocks—with his or her mind cleared of confusion and emptied of bias, so that the facts under consideration may make their distinct impressions.

Some schools of literary criticism have gone so far as to assert that a person reading a work of literature should disregard any information that comes from outside the work itself. For many years, some critics have warned against using the details of an author's biography to understand his or her work, while others have argued against allowing a reader's concerns to influence the interpretation of a piece of literature in any way. Facts outside the work and concerns of the reader supposedly cloud the picture and keep the reader from gaining a clear, objective view of the literary object under study.

Paradise Lost: A Case Study

Arguments for this type of "objective" theory of reading may have an impressive ring to them, but are they true to the realities of our experience as readers? Is it possible for us to set aside our preconceptions and read a poem or story with a completely "open" mind? Is this what we actually do when we read? And if it is not what what we do, does that mean that reading can never be more than a subjective activity?

To see if these standards are either necessary or realistic, we can discuss a work of literature often studied in high school or college— Milton's poem *Paradise Lost,* to which I referred earlier in this chapter. What would it be like, a person might wonder, to read this poem without prior knowledge of it or its subject matter? What would it be like to encounter the opening lines of this poem in a totally "fresh" manner?

> Of Man's first disobedience, and the fruit
> Of that forbidden tree, whose mortal taste
> Brought death into the world, and all our woe,
> With loss of Eden, till one greater Man
> Restore us, and regain the blissful seat,
> Sing Heavenly Muse that on the secret top
> Of Oreb, or of Sinai, didst inspire
> That shepherd, who first taught the chosen seed,
> In the beginning how the Heavens and Earth
> Rose out of Chaos . . .
> 　　　　What in me is dark
> Illumine, what is low raise and support;
> That to the height of this great argument
> I may assert Eternal Providence,
> And justify the ways of God to men. (1–10, 22–26)

On a first reading, these lines might leave a reader puzzled about any number of things—What is "Oreb" and who is the "Heavenly Muse?" Milton was an extraordinarily learned person, and *Paradise Lost* is packed with allusions to classical and Christian sources. The pervasive presence of obscure references is one thing that makes reading *Paradise Lost* so difficult. But though very few people will have had enough training to identify all of Milton's allusions, the Christian student may be able to recognize a number of the biblical references in the poem. For example, some Christian readers will identify Oreb as "Horeb," the mountain Moses mentions in Deuteronomy 4:10 as the place at which God commanded him to assemble the Israelites, while others may recognize the "Heavenly Muse" as Milton's term for the Holy Spirit.

In spite of the difficulties that the obscure allusions present, however, many readers will come to the poem with enough knowledge of the biblical story to decipher some of its references. For example, the opening lines—"Of Man's first disobedience, and the fruit / Of that forbidden tree"—refer to events that many readers can interpret without assistance. Even those readers of *Paradise Lost* who have no commitment to the Christian faith may possess sufficient knowledge of the biblical story of the creation and fall to make sense of the poem's main themes.

In addition, there are other constructive assumptions that a reader might bring to *Paradise Lost.* For example, a knowledge of matters of literary tradition and English history may provide a crucial background to the reading of the poem. Working within a tradition that reached back to Homer and Virgil, Milton had set himself the goal of writing an epic of English history. He supported the Puritan cause in the Civil War and served in Oliver Cromwell's government. Because he believed that the Puritan revolution represented the advent of the Kingdom of God upon earth, Milton originally conceived of his epic as a celebration of the glorious history leading up to the establishment of the Kingdom. When Cromwell died and the Puritan government collapsed, however, Milton was deprived of the subject he had chosen for his epic. In political disgrace and personal ruin, he dramatically revised his thinking about his grand poem. Unable to celebrate Christ's triumphant reign in the Puritan kingdom, he wrote instead a drama about the inner warfare of the human spirit.

Because of their knowledge of the Bible and English history, then, some readers will approach *Paradise Lost* with many preconceptions. That is, such readers will have assumed a great deal about the subject matter of the poem even before they have begun to read it. And yet in spite of the importance of scriptural and historical knowledge for understanding Milton's poem, other kinds of assumptions may prove sufficient for the reader of the poem. Although *Paradise Lost* tells specifically of the fall of Adam and Eve, it is also a story about the universal themes of sin, guilt, suffering, longing, and forgiveness. To understand the importance of such themes, a person does not need specific theological training; an awareness of human desire and frailty may prove sufficient for a sensitive, though limited, reading of *Paradise Lost.*

For example, a person would not need to know much about the Christian faith to comprehend Satan's motives at the beginning of the poem. In many ways, the Devil resembles average men and women—that is, *us*—in his behavior. Magnified in him are typical pettiness, pride, and self-deception. And while the language of the rest of the poem may often be difficult to decipher, Satan's speeches are clear and direct. To understand them, we do not need much more than the general knowledge of human behavior which we bring to the poem. If we comprehend what Satan is saying in his speeches, it may well be because we understand ourselves.

Among other things, we may be able to understand his reckless defiance:

> What though the field be lost?
> All is not lost; the unconquerable will,
> And study of revenge, immortal hate,
> And courage never to submit or yield:
> And what is else not to be overcome?
> That glory never shall his wrath or might
> Extort from me. (105–111)

Or, as Satan contemplates his new home in hell, we may well recognize his arrogance about the power of his mind to give a pleasing shape to his reality:

> Farewell happy fields,
> Where joy for ever dwells: Hail horrors! hail
> Infernal world! and thou profoundest Hell,
> Receive thy new possessor, one who brings
> A mind not to be changed by place or time.
> The mind is its own place, and in itself
> Can make a Heaven of Hell, a Hell of Heaven. (249–255)

Or perhaps we can understand the bitter desperation of his priding himself on the fact that in one day he can undo what it took God six days to make:

> For only in destroying I find ease
> To my relentless thoughts . . .
> To me shall be the glory sole among
> The infernal powers, in one day to have marred
> What he Almighty styled, six nights and days
> Continued making. (ix, 129–30, 135–38)

Because Satan's speeches can be understood without reference to handbooks or dictionaries, they may seem to prove, after all, that a person can read great literature without any assumptions in mind. Yet that is not the case. If we are able to understand the character of Satan, it is because we already know a great deal about desperation, jealousy, and regret. The experiences of our lives make it possible for us to comprehend the experiences we discover in books. They help us construct frameworks to make sense of any new realities we encounter, including the stories, plays, or poems we read. Our assumptions or biases are not impediments to the understanding of a work of literature, but they are what make that understanding possible in the first place. There is no such thing as an "innocent" reading of a book, for every reading is shaped by the biases of the reader.

In *Paradise Lost,* of course, Adam and Eve are supposed to have no biases before their fall. They are innocent. They roam about, naming the animals and enjoying the bounty of God's creation. They *read* nature and experience without *assuming* anything about it:

> Then was not guilty shame; Dishonest shame
> Of Nature's works, honor dishonorable,
> Sin-bred, how have ye troubled all mankind
> With shows instead, mere shows of seeming pure,
> And banished from man's life his happiest life,
> Simplicity and spotless innocence.
> So passed they naked on, nor shunned the sight
> Of God or angel, for they thought no ill;
> So hand in hand they passed, the loveliest pair
> That ever since in love's embraces met:
> Adam the goodliest man of men since born
> His sons, the fairest of her daughters Eve. (313–324)

But there is a vast difference between our situation and that of the inhabitants of Eden, and the fact of that difference is a central point of *Paradise Lost.* We live *after* the fall, and the innocence of Adam and Eve is something we can envy or admire but never experience. Instead, as we read the poem, we experience the dramatic irony of the poem, because we know that Adam and Eve will lose their innocence. The dictionary defines irony as the "incongruity between the actual result of a sequence of events and the normal or expected result"; it points to the gap between *what is* and *what ought to be,* or between *what is* and *what we perceive to be.* Because the reader of *Paradise Lost* knows about the fallen human condition, he or she realizes that the "simplicity and spotless innocence" of Eden will not last.

That is to say that we bring a knowledge of sin and guilt to the reading of any text. Because we are fallen creatures, we never undertake a perfectly unbiased reading of a book. When we meet characters who are "innocent" in their view of reality, we know they will lose that innocence, as our first parents did. Before reading the very first words of a poem or novel, the sensitive reader knows enough of pain, joy, and anxiety to grasp the implications of Satan's warning as he watches the blissful Adam and Eve:

> "Live while ye may,
> Yet happy pair; enjoy, till I return,
> Short pleasures, for long woes are to succeed." (533–535)

What We Do When We Read

What might this discussion of *Paradise Lost* have to teach us about the nature of reading? First, it demonstrates how each of us comes to the act of reading with basic assumptions in mind. As readers, we know something about the subject matter of a book even before we read its opening lines. Contrary to the claims of Shaftesbury and Kant, each of us has an interest in the subject matter of a work of literature as we read it. This means that in reading *Paradise Lost*, we bring to the poem a set of beliefs about the poem's subject matter—about God, the Fall, and sin—and that without these biases, we would not be able to make any sense out of the poem. The biases do not block our path to understanding; instead, they show us where to begin our journey. They enable us to form the questions that begin our dialogue with the poem or work of fiction we are reading.

In that dialogue, some of our preconceptions are confirmed, while others are modified or proven to be false. For example, a reading of *Paradise Lost* reveals that Satan is deceptive and destructive, just as we may have long been told he is. But our reading of the poem may reveal another side to Satan's character. Here, he expresses remorse and shows a form of compassion. As he looks at his fellow fallen angels or gazes at Adam and Eve, Satan is pained to know that he is leading so many to suffering and ruin. This is perhaps not the kind of behavior we expect from the Arch Deceiver, but if we read *Paradise Lost* carefully, we are likely to finish the poem with an altered view of Satan.

We might call the assumptions we bring to our reading of a work *prejudices*. This is a negative term in our age, for it now refers almost exclusively to racial bias or religious bigotry. But in the context of reading, there may be more constructive ways to conceive of prejudice. In the history of the law, prejudice means something very different from the "groundless assumption" or "bias" of our common usage. "In German legal terminology a 'prejudice' is a provisional legal verdict before the final verdict is reached," writes Hans-Georg Gadamer. It is a necessary prejudgment, which is made before all the facts are in; only a rigorous testing of the prejudice can determine whether it is true or false. It was only in the eighteenth century that the word came to mean "unfounded judgment" (240).

Another way of putting this is to say that in every area of thought and judgment, we use hypotheses to make sense of the new facts we discover. The trial judge brings a knowledge of the law into the proceedings of a particular murder case; the chemist brings assumptions about the behavior of molecules into the process of observing what happens in a lab experiment; and the reader of a novel brings some prior knowledge of history and human nature to bear upon the events of an unfolding tale.

To say that "prejudices" play a vital role in our reading is not to say that we are locked in the prison cells of our own subjectivity. Rather, it is to acknowledge that there may be truth in the beliefs of the vast communities, past and present, to which our prejudices connect us. After all, "prejudices can change, but not all prejudices are false; some remain unaffected by the fires of doubt" (Weinsheimer, 12). As the chapters on metaphor and stories pointed out, all words have histories. Any word we use is already charged with meaning when we pick it up to employ it. To a significant extent, we owe our ability to understand anything to those who have gone before us and have given our language the meanings that make sense of things for us.

This is true, for example, in reading the Scriptures. If you sit down to read with nothing but your Bible in front of you, you may think that no one else's ideas influence the way you read the words on the page. But is that true? Would it not be closer to the truth to say that as you read you are influenced by the assumptions you have learned from pastors, teachers, parents, and friends? And in turn, have not those who shaped your understanding also felt the significant influence of others upon them? The writer of the letter to the Hebrews speaks of the great cloud of witnesses surrounding us in the faith. Individual Christians are always part of the larger body of the Church, and the solitary reader of the Bible is always indebted to past and present brothers and sisters in Christ for his or her understanding.

When we read, then, our goal should be, not so much to cast our assumptions aside before we begin, as to test and clarify them to bring them in line with the truth. If our goal is to discover the truth of what we read, we will want to test our prejudices and explore the values of what we are encountering as we read. Our dialogue with the book we are reading and with others who have interpreted it may challenge our cherished beliefs (as Huck Finn's experiences with Jim challenged some of the truths he held most dear). But we could not engage in dialogue if we came to the experience without assumptions of any kind. The person who reads with a completely open mind reads with an empty mind.

Understanding another person or a book is thus not a matter of casting off our own assumptions in order to put on those belonging to someone else. Instead, when we read, we are striving to hear what the other person has said about a subject that matters to us. When I read a novel by Jane Austen or a poem by T. S. Eliot, for example, I can never claim that I have so completely entered the world of their work that I have left my own values completely behind. To understand *Pride and Prejudice,* I do not need to become a woman of forty living in southwestern England at the beginning of the nineteenth century. Nor to hear what Eliot is saying in *The Waste Land* do I need to forget myself and pretend to be an expatriate American living in London immediately after World War I.

In conclusion, we acknowledge that we come to a book like *Paradise Lost* with a good number of assumptions already in mind before we have read even a word of the poem. We have prior beliefs about good and evil, human nature, and matters of freedom and justice. These beliefs or prejudices are what make it possible for us to make any sense whatsoever out of Milton's poem. When we read Milton, we are not trying to *enter his mind* but to *hear* what he has to say.

In addition, we seek to hear what others have said about Milton's work and about the important issues that it discusses. As we enter into a dialogue with any work of literature and its interpreters, we expose our prejudices to scrutiny and may either be challenged or confirmed in our beliefs. In listening to Milton and many other authors and readers, we seek to discern more of the truth than we already know.

Chapter 8

THE CONFLICT OF INTERPRETATIONS

The previous chapter discussed what we do when we read literature, but it did not consider the issue of proper interpretation. If we do not wish to claim that all interpretations of a work are equally valid, how can we discriminate between them? Can we develop the proper methods to get the correct meaning from what we are reading? How do we reconcile belief in the Bible as the clear presentation of God's truth with the fact that sincere Christians have come up with so many contradictory interpretations of passages in it?

For the contemporary Christian reader, these questions about interpretation have roots in the experience of the Reformation. When Wycliffe, Luther, Calvin, and others sought to free themselves from the authority of the Catholic Church, they were resisting among other things the power of the church over biblical interpretation. In the middle ages, Christians employed a great number of methods to interpret the scripture, but the authority to declare an interpretation or method valid belonged to the hierarchy of the Church. For the most part, questions of interpretation had to be treated as questions of authority.

Among other things, the Reformation represented a dramatic shift in Western thinking about interpretation and the question of authority. Martin Luther stated the case simply: "no believing Christian can be forced to recognize any authority beyond the sacred scripture, which is exclusively invested with divine right, unless, indeed, there comes a new and attested revelation" (Grant, 129–30). In both of the great movements of the early modern age, the Renaissance and

Reformation, there was a revolutionary emphasis upon individual rights and powers, which included the right to read the Word of God without the intervention of outside authorities.

Perhaps more than any other factor, this emphasis upon individual liberty created the potential for the conflict of interpretations. Luther argued that *scriptura scripturæ interpres*—that scripture is its own interpreter. He and other Reformers argued for the perspicuity of the Bible. This is the belief that the Bible is so clearly written that, with the aid of the Holy Spirit, all who have saving faith may find its meaning clear. In this line of thought, if disagreements over the meaning of a passage arise, they are due either to a lack of faith on the part of a party to the dispute, or because an interpreter has allowed outside traditions to stand between him or her and the passage in question.

Protestants soon discovered conflicts growing out of their new view of interpretation, however. Luther himself faced difficulties arising from the radical interpretation given to the Bible by participants in the Peasants' Revolt; during the Puritan Revolution in England in the 1640s, radical sects gave provocative readings to key passages of scripture in their battle to seize power from the King and his loyalists; and from the very beginning of Christian life in North America, conflicting interpretations of the Bible proliferated.

The American Scene

The American context is important for an understanding of the conflict of interpretations, because of an American tendency to believe that such conflicts are superficial rather than deeply rooted. After all, since the early days of the settling of the New World, the promise of America has been that in the new land a person could leave behind the inhibiting and binding prejudices of the Old World. In America, men and women are supposedly united by a common faith in a glorious future. In that future, the conflicts of the present will be resolved through the exercise of a spirit of acceptance and understanding.

That last sentence—about "a spirit of acceptance and understand-ing"—sounds vague. But that is the point. The beliefs of the old world had been too clear, many would claim. Trivial matters of theological belief or political conviction had been allowed to divide people and set them at war with one another. In the clear air and open spaces of the New World, the sharp differences that had divided Europe for centuries were supposed to disappear. For example, an eighteenth-century French immigrant to America, St. Jean de Crevecoeur, expressed delight over the fact that in America "the various Christian sects introduced wear out." In America, when one group disapproves of the way another group worships or interprets the Bible, its members simply move to another location "and there worship the Divinity agreeably to their own peculiar ideas. Nobody disturbs them."

In Crèvecoeur's view, freedom means the right to believe and act as you please within your own world. Such an ideal of liberty appeals to those who yearn to be free from the influence of others, and it offers comfort and protection to those who have suffered persecution for their beliefs. But it is not likely to prove satisfying to someone longing to discover a common truth or to belong to a genuine com-munity. Beneath all the exuberant proclamations of personal freedom in American culture, one can hear the lament of people who long for common bonds with one another.

A Christian ideal of freedom must include something more than the right to be different from others. In the image offered by the Apostle Paul, God calls each Christian to worship the truth and to serve the body of Christ. In America, however, the call to Christian unity has often meant that each denomination or body of believers claims its understanding of the scriptures as *the* correct interpretation of the truth. Christians in the New World often seem eager to say, "Yes, all Christians could live together in harmony, if only everyone saw things as we do—rightly, that is." As more than one observer of the American church has noted, convictions of this kind have made genuine communion among Christians difficult in the New World. A perceptive nineteenth-century theologian, John W. Nevin, asked,

But what are we to think of it when we find such a motley mass of protesting systems, all laying claim so vigorously here to one and the same watchword? If the Bible be at once so clear and full as a formulary of Christian doctrine and practice, how does it come to pass that where men are left most free . . . to use it in this way, and have the greatest mind to do so, according to their own profession, they are flung assunder so perpetually in their religious faith, instead of being brought together, by its influence. (Hatch 73–74)

A novelist who struggled with dilemmas of this kind was Nathaniel Hawthorne, the author of *The Scarlet Letter*. Though he was a direct descendant of the Puritans, Hawthorne had mixed feelings about his heritage. On the one hand, he was ashamed enough of the role an ancestor had played in the Salem Witch trials to change his family's name from Hathorne to Hawthorne. But at the same time, Hawthorne knew that his own culture did not have the clear beliefs and strong sense of communal purpose of the first New England settlers. Thus, although he abhorred the injustices of Puritan society, Hawthorne felt drawn to the unifying convictions of the earlier age.

In *The Scarlet Letter*, Hawthorne tried to envision how men and women might come together in common understanding even after they had lost the ability to believe in Christian truth. The plot of the story is familiar even to many who have never read the novel: in seventeenth-century Boston Hester Prynne commits adultery and is forced to stand before the people of the town, with a red-letter "A" upon her dress and with her illegitimate child, Pearl, in her arms. The town does not know the identity of her adulterous accomplice, and she refuses to reveal his name. The action of the novel consists, to a great extent, of the inner struggles of Hester and Arthur Dimmesdale, a highly revered minister and Pearl's father.

In Puritan Boston, adultery was a serious breach of the marriage covenant and a clear violation of the commandment of God. In the novel, the town punishes Hester for having shown a wanton disregard for its values, for having disdained its interpretation of human nature and the law of God. By punishing Hester, the community hopes to make her repent, and thus to bring her to the point where she will share its understanding of the truth. It seeks to make Hester serve as a warning to those who might find themselves tempted in a similar manner. The community operates with the confidence that it can force the proper interpretation of values upon anyone who lives in its midst.

Hester's judges believe deeply in the rightness of their actions and interpretations. "A blessing on the righteous Colony of the Massachusetts, where iniquity is dragged out into the sunshine!" cries the magistrate who leads Hester and her daughter to the scaffold. When Hester refuses to divulge the name of her lover, a minister delivers

to the multitude a discourse on sin, in all its branches, but with continual reference to the ignominious letter. So forcibly did he dwell upon this symbol . . . that it assumed new terrors in their imagination, and seemed to derive its scarlet hue from the flames of the infernal pit.

Throughout the novel, the letter means one thing for the Puritan community and another for Hester. For Boston, the "A" stands for adultery, a lurid and shameful deed whose consequences are evil. For Hester and her partner in sin, however, the "A" has other meanings. Hester's sinful experience and her wearing of the scarlet letter seem to have given her new categories of understanding. Cut off from the community, she "felt or fancied . . . that the scarlet letter had endowed her with a new sense. . . . It gave her a sympathetic knowledge of the hidden sin in other hearts." As she guesses the secrets hidden in the hearts of others, Hester finds herself tempted to believe "that the outward guise of purity was but a lie, and that, if truth were everywhere to be shown, a scarlet letter would blaze forth on many a bosom besides Hester Prynne's."

The longer she wears the scarlet letter, the more complete her estrangement becomes. "The effect of the symbol . . . on the mind of Hester Prynne herself, was powerful and peculiar," Hawthorne writes. Hester conforms outwardly, but inwardly her heart is in turmoil as she contemplates the meaning of the emblem. She finds every conviction thrown into question, and she even wonders whether it might be best for her to "send Pearl at once to heaven, and go herself to such futurity as Eternal Justice should provide." Faced with clear evidence that Hester has hardly come around to the Puritan interpretation of experience, Hawthorne concludes that "the scarlet letter had not done its office!"

Arthur Dimmesdale faces similar difficulties. It becomes almost impossible for him to live with his own dishonesty and with the deceitfulness he finds to be at the heart of Puritan culture. Trained to worship purity and the truth, Arthur must acknowledge that he and his community are impure and deceitful. The glorious interpretation he gives to experience in his sermons is praised by his parishioners, but it is very far from the truth. Dimmesdale finds the discrepancy between appearance and reality to be unbearable; he is all but crushed by his own hypocrisy.

Seeking release, he stumbles out to the scaffolding one night to "confess" his crime. While standing there, he witnesses the fall of a meteor in the sky. "Nothing was more common, in those days," Hawthorne writes, "than to interpret all meteoric appearances, and other natural phenomena, that occurred with less regularity than the rise and set of sun and moon, as so many revelations from a supernatural source."

We impute it, therefore, solely to the disease in his own eye and heart, that the minister, looking upward to the zenith, beheld there the appearance of an immense letter,—the letter A,—marked out in lines of dull red light. Not but the meteor may have shown itself at that point, burning duskily through a veil of cloud; but with no such shape as his guilty imagination gave it; or, at least, with so little definiteness, that another's guilt might have seen another symbol in it.

For Reverend Dimmesdale the "A" in the sky is further evidence of his own agonizing guilt. But to the people of Boston, the meteor means something else entirely. The morning after Dimmesdale has stood on the scaffold, the sexton of his church tells him of the "great red letter in the sky—the letter A,—which we interpret to stand for Angel. For as our good Governor [Winthrop] was made an angel this past night, it was doubtless held fit that there should be some notice thereof!"

Conflicting interpretations of this sort abound throughout the novel. In a climactic scene, Hester urges Arthur to flee with her from Boston, to throw off the system of belief which condemns and weighs them down. But Arthur Dimmesdale cannot fulfill his promise to leave, and as the novel nears its end, he mounts the scaffold for a final time. Having planned to confess, he cries out, "Stand any here that question God's judgment on a sinner? Behold! Behold a dreadful witness of it!" He then rips open his shirt to reveal the mystery of his sin, and he dies.

But even in confession, Reverend Dimmesdale cannot seem to come upon a common interpretation of symbols and events, one that all members of his community can share. Many witnesses claim to have seen the "A" on Dimmesdale's breast, but among them there is great disagreement; some saw it as an emblem of his self-sacrificing attempt to identify with poor Hester, while others read it as a sign inflicted upon him by the wicked wizard, Roger Chillingworth, and still others viewed it as a manifestation of an inward guilt that had finally gnawed its way out. But some "highly respectable witnesses" claim to have seen nothing at all on Dimmesdale's chest. According to them,

After exhausting life in his efforts for mankind's spiritual good, he had made the manner of his death a parable, in order to impress on his admirers the mighty and mournful lesson, that, in the view of Infinite Purity, we are sinners all alike.

For these particular witnesses, a confession of adultery was the last thing Dimmesdale could possibly have been making.

In two famous essays published about a decade before *The Scarlet Letter*, Hawthorne's contemporary, Ralph Waldo Emerson, urged his American audience to trust its instincts in all phases of life—in its reading habits as well as its actions. "If the single man plant himself indomitably upon his instincts, and there abide, the huge world will come round to him," Emerson promised in "The American Scholar." "To believe your own thought," in effect, to believe your own interpretation of a text or event, "to believe that what is true for you in your private heart, is true for all men,—that is genius. Speak your latent conviction, and it shall be the universal sense," he claimed in "Self-Reliance."

We might say that *The Scarlet Letter* represents Hawthorne's failed attempt to realize this great Emersonian promise for American life. In the novel, the characters do not successfully exchange their blinding prejudices for enlightened understanding. They never do see the same thing in the symbol of the "A." The Puritans fail in their efforts to make Hester conform to their vision of experience, and the community refuses to change its cherished interpretations of human actions and symbols. Instead, they persist in reading into the scarlet letter their deeply rooted prejudices, and spend most of their time embellishing beliefs they already hold.

Thus, for Hawthorne the promise of America—that in a land of freedom, decent men and women can discard their prejudices and share an innocent vision of life—becomes a tragic illusion. The romantic poets and essayists such as Emerson had promised that shared symbols could free us from our painfully limited perceptions. The conflicts between different schools of thought and different theological positions would vanish when, like Adam and Eve in the Garden of Eden, we once again gazed upon reality with innocent eyes. Hawthorne came to realize, reluctantly, that such innocent reading is forever behind us.

Hawthorne realized the unavoidable truth that, as the previous chapter pointed out, we read our books and our experiences with preconceptions in place even before we begin the work of conscious interpretation. It is naive to think that we can set aside our prejudices with ease, for we are bound to the past more than we know and more than some of the Reformers and Romantic poets may have realized. Because of the strength of traditions and the depth of our differing convictions, it is hardly surprising that we come up with conflicting interpretations when we read. What is more surprising is that, in spite of our prejudices and traditions, we are able to come to agreement with one another on so many issues.

How Do We Resolve These Things?

For many Christians, however, it is difficult at times to detect the grace of God at work amidst the confusion of interpretive disagreements. What do we do if and when the experience of *The Scarlet Letter* becomes our experience? That is, how do we deal with the competing claims of conflicting interpretations? Though our first inclination may be to believe there is but one correct interpretation of a book or an event—and that we are the ones who have discovered the right reading—what do we do if our confidence in our ability to find that right interpretation wears off?

In seeking to understand how to proceed once we have lost that confidence, we might begin by questioning the belief that there is a single correct interpretation of a work of literature. The Christian can believe that in the mind of God there is a single, unified truth about any book, event, or human action. But none of us possesses the mind of God. As the Apostle Paul tells us, we see through a glass darkly, and only in the kingdom of the Risen Christ will we see face to face (1 Corinthians 13). When we study a work of literature intently, we may hear or see a portion of the truth, but we do not grasp it fully, not in this life at least.

The Christian reader needs to distinguish between the question of truth and the question of understanding. Though the truth is one, our comprehension is partial. When we interpret, we try to discover the meaning of the truth, and though the truth remains the same, the implications of an action or book may vary through time and from place to place. Our understanding of a book or event develops and grows because we can discover things we had overlooked in our earlier interpretation of it. As we learn new things about it, the significance of a book may deepen for us.

One way of putting it might be to say that in the drama of history, each of us—as an author of books or experiences and as an interpreter—plays a part in a much larger story being told by God. In playing our individual parts, we contribute to the action and meaning of the entire drama, but as characters, none of us is capable of serving as the author of the whole play, nor is any one of us able to give the exhaustive meaning of the much larger story in which we each have a role to play.

The Danish writer of fiction, Isak Dinesen, returned repeatedly to such themes in her stories. (Isak Dinesen is the pen name of Karen Blixen, whose early life was chronicled in the movie *Out of Africa.*) At the center of one of her stories, "The Roads Round Pisa," Dinesen places a character named Count Augustus von Schimmelmann. The count is a melancholy Danish man who is traveling towards the city of Pisa in 1823. As the story opens, Count Augustus is pondering the question of truth, and like many northern European characters in Dinesen's fiction, he is obsessed with the possibility of the individual's solitary discovery of that truth. "How difficult it is to know the truth. I wonder if it is really possible to be absolutely truthful when you are alone." The truth about this road, he concludes, "is that it leads to Pisa, and the truth about Pisa can be found within books written and read by human beings" (165).

Yet in spite of his doubts about the possibility of knowing the truth in solitude, Count Augustus finds it too difficult to break free of his preoccupation with his own story. In "The Roads Round Pisa," Dinesen immerses her readers in a series of interconnecting stories. In mysterious ways, many of the characters who meet along this road turn out to have ties to the "stories" of one another's lives. At one point, the Count comes upon a puppet comedy being put on at an inn near Pisa. At the end of the comedy, the character of "the witch appears again, and on being asked what is really the truth, answers: 'The truth, my children, is that we are, all of us, acting in a marionette comedy. What is important more than anything else in a marionette comedy, is keeping the ideas of the author clear. This is the real happiness of life. . . .' " To the Count, all the people of this southern "country seemed, somehow, to be practicing this ideal." The Count and his fellow northerners are afflicted by "strong agitations of the soul" and find their speech coming to them "by fits and starts." To the people of the South, on the other hand, it seemed "as if life were, in any of her whims, a comedy which they had already rehearsed" (199).

At the very end of the story, Count Augustus discovers a remarkable fact that reveals his own connection to the many stories that have been spun around him on the road to Pisa. But rather than share that fact with anyone else, he hoards it. It was "something which was meant for him only . . . and which he could not share with anybody else any more than he would be able to share his dreams." And at the very end of the story, we find him "taking a small mirror from his pocket. Holding it in the flat of his hand, he looked thoughtfully into it" (216). What Augustus has failed to learn in spite of the evidence he has been given, the critic Robert Langbaum claims, is "that you do not find out who you are by introspection, by looking into a mirror, but by putting on a mask and engaging in an action with such intensity that you step from a human story into God's story" (19).

Dinesen's story points to the fact that though others may have read a story or poem in a way very different from our own interpretation, this is not in itself a threat to our belief in the truth. We learn the truth about a book by attending very carefully to its details—to what it says and the way it says it. We observe and listen to the work closely and consider it in terms that we can understand. And then, we enter into conversation with others about it. We listen to what others in the past have said about it and we turn to hear what those around us at present have to say in response.

As we engage in this "conversation" about the work, we keep in mind that differing interpretations of the same book or action may complement each other without necessarily contradicting one another. When an orchestra performs Brahms's *Symphony No. 2,* for example, the violas, cellos, and horns all have their separate parts to play. If they do it right, what comes out of their playing is a harmonious whole which is more than the sum of its parts. Each performer has a specific part to play in the larger production. The performance would not work if everyone played the same notes, or if each instrumentalist disobeyed the score and played whatever notes came to his or her mind. Just as we would not criticize an oboist for playing a different part from a trombonist, so too should we be careful not to dismiss immediately those whose interpretations differ from our own.

In interpreting written works, Paul Ricoeur argues, we have the opportunity to discover the multiple ways in which our lives are dependent upon forces greater than our selves. Developments in philosophy and psychology over the past century have shown us how much *unconscious* meaning there is in our actions; as a result, the meaning of a poem or novel may well involve a discussion of the inner conflicts of the author or the underlying struggles of the society in which the work first appeared. When interpreting a work of literature, we also pay heed to the matter of the *conscious* meaning that we as humans give to our actions through our setting of goals and our adhering to standards; in reading a play or a novel, this may include asking questions about the author's moral values and his or her artistic goals in composing the work. And finally, there is, in Ricoeur's categories, the vast realm of the *sacred* which imparts meaning to our lives and deeply influences the interpretations Christians have of events; for the Christian critic, attention to matters of the sacred may include a concern for the theological significance of a work of literature, and it may mean that the Christian reader judges the work in the light of his or her deepest convictions.

Each of these realms reveals something of the full meaning of our experience. An interpretation focusing upon only one aspect of human experience would disclose the truth of the work to a limited extent. I can well imagine, for example, that a Christian reading of *The Scarlet Letter* might rely on Freudian thought to discover part of the truth of that work. I cannot imagine a Christian interpretation which would claim that the Freudian reading disclosed the ultimate insight about the work.

In other words, the Christian living in the modern world can affirm that the full meaning of any text or action is neither single nor limitless. It is not valid to say that a poem means one thing and one thing only nor that it means whatever we want it to mean. We can say a number of true things about a work of literature, but not everything we say is necessarily true. There are meanings to a work of literature that complement one another by revealing the possible implications of a work. But there are also meanings that contradict one another, and they present the more difficult problem for the Christian longing to know and serve the truth.

How do we discover that truth? We discover it by the slow and arduous task of weighing any interpretation against what we already hold to be the truth about the matter in question. In addition, we question whether there is any evidence in the work for the claims that are being made about it. In the case of a work of literature, this involves testing the interpretation against the evidence given within the work itself and the knowledge we may have of the author's life and the historical context of the work. (Did Hawthorne really struggle with an image of a harsh and distant father and a similar image of God? In his fiction, does Hawthorne give any evidence of being aware of the similarities between himself and Dimmesdale?)

We also discover the truth by testing our reading of the work through a dialogue with those of like mind and those likely to disagree with us. As we struggle with ourselves and with one another, we keep before us the hope that the truth will be revealed more fully. If we study history, we discover that this is the way that the implications of the truth have often emerged—in the debates of Church councils, in the give and take of political dealings, and in extended discussions about powerful books or works of art. Issues that may seem very settled to us from a safe distance were most often resolved only after long, difficult debate.

If you look back at your own life, you may well find that your understanding of the truth about yourself has emerged in a similar way. In the slow process of the years, your identity has become more complex to you, and you understand yourself in a far different way than you did when you were ten years old. No doubt, by the time you reach thirty or forty years of age, even more things will have been added to your understanding of the meaning of your life.

That does not mean that truth cannot appear to us in other ways. After all, Paul was struck down on the Damascus Road, and Jesus called his disciples to come to him immediately. (But even there, did it not take some of the disciples a very long time to have the truth of Christ finally dawn on them?) Yes, truth can come in a flash. But when we live in a culture that yearns for everything—including the discovery of the truth—to be instantaneous, it is good to remind ourselves that the conflict between our different visions of the truth is itself as old as history.

As we search for the truth and long to be reconciled to one another, we can take heart in the promises of God. I am thinking here of the repeated promises in the Scripture that God knows us better than we know ourselves. The clarity with which God sees us is much greater than our vision of him. We are called to the difficult task of discerning the truth, but at the same time we are reminded that we are, in a very real sense, only children at play in God's kingdom. We laugh and dispute and long to know the truth. And though our experience is often one of conflict, including the conflict of interpretations, as Christians we also have a genuine hope:

How great is the love the Father has lavished on us, that we should be called children of God! And that is what we are! The reason the world does not know us is that it did not know him. Dear friends, now we are children of God, and what we will be has not yet been made known. But we know that when he appears, we shall be like him, for we shall see him as he is. Everyone who has this hope in him purifies himself, just as he is pure. (1 John 3:1–3)

PART 3

How Should We Select and
Evaluate What We Read?

Chapter 9

THE VALUE AND LIMITS OF READING THE CLASSICS

The three leading fast-food franchisers spent half a billion dollars in 1986 to advertise their products. McDonald's introduced its McDLT delivered in a divided styrofoam container; Burger King emphasized its flame-broiling technique to appeal to the customer searching for a low-fat product. Given the success of these marketing strategies, Wendy's needed to strike back, so it conducted extensive taste tests experimenting with catsup, mustard, onions, and pickle-placement to come up with the exact formula consumers preferred. Not content to depend on this widespread market testing and perhaps aware that the new burger strongly resembled their old "Single," Wendy's christened the new creation "The Big Classic." "This is the good stuff," their television jingles intoned.

Wendy's advertising designers saw the new name of their burger as a way to point to the high quality of their product. Like that other well-known classic, an automobile built before 1942, their classic was good and was enduring. They ignored the irony that it was also new. Like Wendy's, most introductory literature courses feature "the good stuff": the literary classics or masterpieces, as these works are often called in course titles.

A classic work, according to *Webster's New World Dictionary*, is one "of the highest class; being a model of its kind; excellent; standard; authoritative; established." Applied to cars or hamburgers, the term becomes a normative judgment of the enduring excellence of the product. Both quality and longevity contribute to the formation of a classic.

During the Renaissance, literary scholars saw Greek and Roman epic and drama as the best examples of good literature, modelling the qualities which other literature should attempt to achieve. Consequently, a *classic* came to be known in its narrow sense as a literary work of ancient Greece or Rome. However, in a wider sense it now refers to any work generally considered to be of the highest rank or excellence. Courses called "American Literary Classics" or "Masterpieces of World Literature" look at literary works that have historically been defined as some of the best. This is the good stuff.

Those works that numerous scholars of Western culture believe to be classics, representing some of the best literature ever written, make up what we call the *literary canon*. In order to establish a canon, some kind of authority decides whether to include or exclude a work. The biblical canon, with which we are now so familiar, was established by the authority of the early church, which accepted the Gospels of Matthew, Mark, Luke, and John, but rejected the Gospel of Thomas. A less clearly defined authority creates the literary canon, and, unlike the biblical canon, it is the subject of continuing debate and evaluation. No specific group of literary scholars ever met to decide what works would or would not be included. Writers, readers, and critics continually debate which works and authors are the best. Classic works are those which have been continually celebrated, analyzed, and discussed by successive generations of trained readers.

As canons are formed, they become part of the institutionalization of literature. The standard works and authors taught in graduate schools, researched and written about in scholarly journals and books, and subsequently included in textbooks such as those issued by Norton, Macmillan, Oxford, Harper & Row, or Little, Brown are the current version of the canon.

The Value of the Canon

Although its origin is informal and its contents at times ambiguous, a canon unquestionably exists. Certain authors and works have a longstanding and honored place in the canon. To a certain extent, we can identify a particular work as being in or out of the canon. Shakespeare is in; Stephen King is out. This does not mean that Stephen King does not write literature; it only means that he does not write works of a kind that most literary scholars would term "good literature."

Most of the literature taught in high-school and college courses comes from the current canon, and for good reason. This canon is a collection of some of the highlights of Western thought; it includes what many people believe to be "the best that is known and thought in the world," in the words of the English essayist Matthew Arnold. Many of the great works of literature that can enrich our lives are found in the canon and are part of our commonly shared culture.

Reading the works of literature that make up the canon can assist us in accomplishing our Christian vocation. The works of the canon speak great wisdom about what it means to be a human being. They contain profound ways of thinking about the significance of life and its problems. We can learn important truths if we listen to what the canon has to say. Furthermore, the canon contains works of stunning beauty and skill in which we can delight.

Familiarity with literary classics also helps us to comprehend Western culture more fully. A knowledge of the canon is essential if we wish to understand ourselves as individuals situated within a particular culture, for the canon is a historical record of that culture. As we learn how meanings, metaphors, and narratives have developed and influenced our own society and culture, we can learn how to love and serve our neighbors better. Studying the canon allows us both to reject our culture's incorrect ideas and to learn from its wisdom.

The canon has a continued impact on culture as it influences new literary works. As the British novelist Virginia Woolf writes, "Masterpieces are not single and solitary births; they are the outcome of many years of thinking in common, of thinking by the body of the people, so that the experience of the mass is behind the single voice" (68–69).

Familiarity with Shakespeare's *King Lear* helps us to understand Melville's *Moby-Dick,* which helps us to understand *Star Trek 3: The Wrath of Khan* (to use a nonliterary example). Each subsequent work draws on the imagery, rhetoric, characters, and philosophy of an earlier work. Lear's despair and questioning of God enhance Melville's portrait of Captain Ahab even as Khan adopts the crazed poetic monomania of Ahab to justify his own doomed pursuit of the *Enterprise*.

Knowing the canon, then, helps us to understand other texts' allusions, common themes, and culturally developed metaphors and concepts. Studying the canon makes us culturally literate, able to read and interpret the numerous texts produced daily in our society. If we are to use the textual power of literature wisely to improve God's world, we need to have this kind of literacy.

The Danger of the Canon

The creation of a literary canon, however, also results in many problems. We need to understand its true nature in order to avoid either sanctifying it or employing it unfairly to exclude other writing not of canonical status. Although God orders history to preserve many good gifts for us through tradition, not everything preserved is beneficial, excellent, or valuable. We may find some works in the canon to be harmful and discover that other good gifts of literature have been excluded.

How could this kind of exclusion happen? The canon was put together very informally through the work of literary scholars, who were primarily white, upper-class, Western European men. Consequently, it was shaped by their tastes, preferences, and judgments. In canonizing certain works as "timeless" and "universally great," these men tended to choose a certain kind of literature and to omit other kinds less familiar to them. Literary scholar H. Bruce Franklin explains:

It [the canon] substitutes a tiny part for the whole, demeaning as subliterary or otherwise unworthy of serious attention almost the entire body of the world's literature, especially popular literature (including science fiction, detective stories, westerns, and tales of adventure and romance), folk literature, oral literature, literature based on the experience of work, especially industrial work and domestic work, and almost all literature by nonwhite peoples. (96)

As recently as thirty years ago, the canon included few women and even fewer black, native American, or Third-World writers.

These absences cannot be explained completely by the lack of material written by members of these marginal groups, but can in part be attributed to the limited critical and cultural vision of those in positions of literary authority. The English professors from Oxford, Cambridge, Harvard, and Yale never met together and schemed to exclude all black or women authors, but the canon did evolve from the scholarly work of men who often did not value the voices and strategies of other less privileged groups.

Deciding what represents the best, the most excellent, the highest class of literature is unquestionably a value judgment, even though many of the creators of the canon often defended their selections by claiming such works were eternal, timeless, universal, and self-evidently the masterpieces of literature. A quick overview of the formation of a canon, however, shows how literary values can shift and remold it.

Adalaide Morris, a professor of English at the University of Iowa, found major changes occurring in the American literary canon over the last eighty-five years when she examined the contents of standard anthologies. She reports that the anthologies "record surges of fashion as fixed certainties." In the 1920s, the "in" authors included Longfellow, Bryant, Whittier, Holmes, and Hawthorne. The 1950s registered a new surge. All of the previous giants except Hawthorne were "out," their pages in the anthologies severely reduced, their works less frequently written about and discussed. The new topics of attention were Emerson, Thoreau, Poe, Whitman, Melville, and Dickinson (470–72).

Canonical changes continue to occur in the 1980s as scholars identify the prejudices of the canon and work to correct these errors by including more non-white American and women writers in new anthologies. The second edition of *The Norton Anthology of American Literature,* published in 1985, explains in its Preface, "A major responsibility of this Norton anthology is to redress the long neglect of women writers in America. . . . Another responsibility is to do justice to the contributions of black writers to American literature and culture." Similar changes are occurring in the British canon.

A study of the canon shows that literary scholars have often changed their minds about what the best works of literature are. Indeed, these changes in the canon arise because of shifting ideas about what constitutes good literature. The changes in the American anthologies noted by Professor Morris occurred because in the 1920s critics valued elegance, wit, formal verse, and skillful use of conventions, while the critics of the 1940s admired experimental, doubtful, pessimistic, or paradoxical writing. When evaluating texts, critics today often look for political implications, social statements, or effective depictions of personal experience.

Uncle Tom's Cabin, published in 1852 by Harriet Beecher Stowe, provides an excellent example of the way the evaluation of a work can change. The novel vividly depicts the destruction of black family life by the institution of slavery and issues a strong emotional and religious appeal for the abolition of slavery. In its own time, *Uncle Tom's Cabin* was the most popular American novel, far surpassing Melville's *Moby-Dick* (1851) or Hawthorne's *The Scarlet Letter* (1850), and becoming the first American novel to sell over a million copies. Yet throughout most of the twentieth century, *Uncle Tom's Cabin* was excluded from the literary canon and scorned as "sentimental" and "artless."

The recent campaign to establish this novel as part of the canon has been led by Jane P. Tompkins, who argues that the work of sentimental nineteenth-century writers is complex, significant, and resourceful, but employs strategies and ideas different from those of Hawthorne and Melville. Tompkins points out that Stowe's novel "insists on religious conversion as the necessary precondition for sweeping social change" and that Stowe organizes her narrative, draws her characters, and employs Biblical rhetoric to depict an urgent need for such conversion (132).

Many modern critics see the world depicted in *Uncle Tom's Cabin* as "naive and unrealistic," since they believe only political and economic action can cause social change. Unable to grasp or accept the novel's premise that religious conversion can prompt social change, such critics deplore its narrative, characters, and language as naive, unrealistic, and unconvincing.

Tompkins's rereading of *Uncle Tom's Cabin* asks us to examine the book on its own terms instead of asking it to resemble Hawthorne's or Melville's style. Stowe uses different kind of techniques skillfully, Tompkins argues, and her novel is a classic in its own right.

Christians and the Canon

The critical misfortunes of *Uncle Tom's Cabin* suggest one of the reasons we need to understand the composition and flaws of the literary canon. Especially since the demise of a Christian cultural consensus in the eighteenth century, texts with strong Christian statements or beliefs have been undervalued and misunderstood by the primarily secular critical community. Often these negative judgments, as in the case of Stowe's novel, are based on inappropriate critical standards.

Donald Davie, the distinguished poet and editor of *The New Oxford Book of Christian Verse*, has devoted much of his scholarly life to exposing the unjust neglect of much Christian verse, especially the genre of the hymn. Davie argues that Christian verse has often been misjudged because it employs a different kind of artistry. He writes:

Talk of "artistry" will mislead us, if it suggests that we ought to look especially for poems that are formally sumptuous and elaborate. On the contrary . . . in every age Christian poets, when they tried to write sacred poems, have fallen in with those theories of poetry which, from the Ancients to the present day, put a specially high value on what is called "the *plain* style," in which elaboration is avoided. (xviii–xix)

The eighteenth-century British poet Isaac Watts provides an excellent example. The author of numerous hymns, including "When I survey the wondrous cross" and "O God, our help in ages past," Watts has received little literary attention. Employing an artistic standard that prizes complexity, critics complain that Watts's lyrics lack bold metaphors or a challenging vocabulary. However, Watts carefully employed the plain style so that his congregation could understand and confess every line as they sang his poems. Given the liturgical function of Watts's verse, a simple style is far more appropriate. Davie suggests that modern criticism has been unable to deal with this kind of poem, and he demonstrates convincingly the skill Watts needed to craft his poetry to succeed as a hymn.

Faced with the biases of the traditional canon, some Christian teachers have chosen to supplement standard textbooks with neglected works. Some have added sections on the hymn as a verse form to their British Literature surveys or their Introduction to Literature courses. Teachers of fiction or drama may deliberately include contemporary short stories or plays written by Christians, which are often overlooked by twentieth-century literary critics. Understanding the genesis of the literary canon may allow us to go beyond its limits and give us the freedom to appreciate and recover parts of the Christian literary tradition that have been needlessly hidden from us.

Recovering the Oppressed

While the narrow vision of the canon has sometimes worked to exclude Christian literary forms or texts with Christian ideas, an even greater injustice has been done to members of oppressed groups: women, ethnic minority, and Third-World authors. After all, for much of cultural history, Christians and Christianity dominated Western thought, and the classics of English literature include works written by Christians such as Donne, Milton, T. S. Eliot, and William Bradford. Women authors have been less fairly represented. Their literary works have often been considered as inferior to those of men, and their own styles, strategies, and forms neglected, even as the hymn form has been. One of the reasons twentieth-century critics took the religion in *Uncle Tom's Cabin* less seriously, Tompkins points out, was because it was associated with women and domesticity.

Beginning in the 1970s, feminist critics began to examine the long-overlooked field of women's writings. As Elaine Showalter explains:

The focus on women's writing as a specific field of inquiry . . . led to a massive recovery and rereading of literature by women from all nations and historical periods. As hundreds of lost women writers were rediscovered, as letters and journals were brought to light, as new literary biographies explored the relationship between the individual female talent and the literary tradition, the continuities in women's writing became clear for the first time. (6)

Similarly overlooked has been the rich tradition of black literature, from spirituals sung in cotton fields, to nineteenth-century autobiographies, to the achievements of Langston Hughes, Gwendolyn Brooks, Zora Neale Hurston, and Linda Brent. Furthermore, the limited approach of the traditional canon means that few of us read works from Asia, South America, or Africa, even in our Masterpieces of World Literature courses, which tend to focus on Western literature.

We should read works excluded by the canon for the same reasons we should read any literature: to expand our vision of reality, to hear the voices of our neighbors and the truths they speak, to appreciate aesthetic excellence. However, we need to break out of our self-centered focus on our own nation, literature, and tradition to explore more widely and learn about our situation in culture as compared to others. Christians should also have a special concern to recover the literature of minorities. The responsibility to promote justice, to satisfy the needs of the oppressed, to identify with the sorrowful impels Christians to attempt to recover the literature of the oppressed.

The prophetic books of the Old Testament give many instructions about Christian responsibility for the oppressed and needy. Christians are to "maintain justice and do what is right" (Isaiah 56:1) and to "satisfy the needs of the oppressed" (Isaiah 58:10). We are "to loose the chains of injustice and untie the cords of the yoke, to set the oppressed free and break every yoke" (Isaiah 58:6). One way to assist the oppressed is to listen to their voices and to hear their concerns. Reading Langston Hughes's "Young Gal's Blues," an anonymous Polish Solidarity protest poem, or the suppressed novel of a Russian dissident, allows us to understand particular forms of oppression better, to sympathize, and to learn how to take action to help others. To acknowledge the literary worth of noncanonical works is a step toward artistic justice.

Recovering the literature of the oppressed also allows us to share in their sorrow. Jesus' first two beatitudes teach that those who are poor in spirit, those who are sorrowful and mourning, are blessed. Eventually they will be comforted, and they will receive the kingdom of heaven. Jesus calls us to experience poverty in spirit and to display a mournful attitude in the same way that he advises us to practice meekness, to hunger for righteousness, to act mercifully, and to be peacemakers.

Jesus' own example teaches us to mourn: faced with the grief of Mary and Martha over Lazarus's death, Jesus wept, even though he knew their brother would shortly be alive again. In Romans 12:15 Paul advises, "Rejoice with those who rejoice; mourn with them who mourn." In these passages the Scriptures seem to indicate our responsibility to grieve in empathy.

Reading literature that reveals the physical and mental conditions of oppression helps us to be sorrowful. The emotions and situations of characters in fictional texts illuminate those in real life. Perusing newspaper accounts about the conditions in the black townships of South Africa, gathering statistics about the distribution of wealth and land, watching on television nightly as riot police beat and arrest black protestors—none of these acts brings home the anguish and oppression of the South African people in quite the same way as reading Alan Paton's *Cry, the Beloved Country,* or Alex La Guma's *A Walk on the Dark Side,* or Athol Fugard's *"Master Harold" and the Boys.* We quickly become numbed by data and historical facts. A textbook account of the Nazi murder of more than six million Jews during World War II provides us with some unbelievable and horrifying information; Elie Wiesel's *Night* causes us to mourn for the victims of the Holocaust.

Reading the literature of the oppressed helps readers in a special way to broaden their knowledge of and response to the world into which God has placed them. Consequently, many Christians will want to go beyond the canon in their reading. The appendix of this book contains some suggestions for beginning to read beyond the canon.

Should We Read Popular Literature?

Works that are read and enjoyed by mass numbers of people are known as *popular literature.* The popular success of an author does not necessarily mean that he or she will be excluded from the canon; Shakespeare, Charles Dickens, and Charlotte Brontë are all highly esteemed in the literary canon, but also were extremely popular in their own time. However, most works of popular culture, such as the science fiction of H. G. Wells, the fantasies of J. R. R. Tolkien, and the mysteries of Agatha Christie, are excluded from the canon.

Even if you are the kind of person who never reads a book, you probably enjoy the most common kind of popular literature around today: television. Although it does not communicate through the medium of writing, television has become the twentieth-century version of oral literature as families nightly gather together around what media expert Quentin Schultze calls "the major storyteller of our age" (18). The particular issues associated with television lie outside the realm of this book, but the visual text of television employs interpretation, metaphor, and narrative in many of the same ways that a written text does.

What is the value of popular literature for the Christian reader? Should we be reading these kinds of works? Literature performs various functions, as we considered earlier. It can entertain as well as deliver a message; it can enlarge our joy as well as enlarge our vision; it can allow us to escape our real-life situation as well as plunge us deeper into our contemporary world and its problems. Not all literature performs every function, and we should not expect it to.

The primary function of most popular literature is entertainment. We may learn something about the French Revolution from a well-researched historical romance, or we may understand our own attitudes about men and women better by reading science fiction set in a world without sexes (as in Ursula K. Le Guin's *The Left Hand of Darkness*), but popular literature's main goal is to provide enjoyment. Other kinds of literature may also be entertaining, but their primary function usually is much more complex.

We all have favorite forms of escapist reading. When I go to the beach or need an airplane book, I prefer to read a traditional murder mystery, complete with a small English village, some shabby gentle-folk, a village church and rector, and, of course, a detective puzzling over a corpse. You may prefer the terrors provided by Stephen King, the fantasy world created by Stephen Donaldson, or the suspense evoked by Tom Clancy. What people find entertaining and relaxing varies with their tastes.

Entertainment, relaxation, enjoyment are all gifts of God to his people. Reading literature that provides these good things is one way we enjoy God's gift of rest. While we would look askance at someone who rested or partied seven days a week, so, too, we may disapprove of a steady diet of popular literature. Given its own purpose and goals, popular literature certainly has a proper place in our reading lives. When we read for pleasure, though, we should not forget about interpretation and evaluation. Popular literature needs a Christian reader just as much as other kinds of literature. Evaluation is still important, and the issues involved in reading discussed throughout this book apply to popular as well as canonical literature.

The Need for Variety

There is value in reading many different kinds of literature. To become acquainted with the classic works of the canon, to explore the neglected writings of the oppressed, and to relax with works of popular literature are all important and worthwhile reading activities. An introductory course in literature helps especially in learning how to read and so to enjoy the works of the canon. Taking a course in literature can also introduce you to works of literature with which you may not be as familiar: world literature, the classics, black literature, or women's literature.

In putting together a personality profile, some reporters like to ask, "If you were abandoned on a desert island and could take only one book with you, what would it be?" Robinson Crusoe was quite disappointed to discover that the sole book he managed to salvage from his shipwreck was the Bible, although in the long run, the Scriptures served him well, effecting his salvation.

If, besides the Bible, you could read only one book in your life, I would tell you to read Melville's *Moby-Dick.* Other people might recommend *The Inferno, King Lear, Paradise Lost, Middlemarch, The Scarlet Letter,* or *Invisible Man.* A well-written epic or novel may provide more beauty and truth, more historical and cultural insight, more questions to ponder, than a simple four-line lyric poem or an entertaining suspense novel.

However, we have a lifetime in which to read and the privilege of choosing a wide variety of material. Sometimes we can read *Moby-Dick,* other times a simple lyric, and other times the Narnia Chronicles. God has given us a world full of possibilities. We can glorify him through many different kinds of reading. Within our personal reading, we should strive for variety and deliberately place ourselves in new reading experiences. If your usual choice is science fiction, perhaps you should try Greek drama, Romantic poetry, or a Russian novel. But we must also realize that each person has different tastes and different talents, and we should not be ashamed of developing areas of personal preference and expertise.

The Christian community as a whole, however, should try to have members reading and evaluating many kinds of literature. In exploring the vast expanses of literature, we need travelers in every field, investigators into every function. By confining ourselves as a community to reading C. S. Lewis and Flannery O'Connor, extolling T. S. Eliot, and searching for works with Christian messages, we will neglect the bounty of good works and the variety of ways that literature can benefit us.

We should neither uncritically accept nor cynically reject the value of the traditional canon. Those who participated in its formation chose much that is good, but left out much of value. We need to be aware of those processes by which canons are constructed and to develop more flexible and expanded ones. That may involve making difficult choices, for when we include some works on a reading list, we exclude others. However, if we want to pursue justice and truth as readers, we need to wrestle with this difficult issue.

Chapter 10

WAS THIS AUTHOR A CHRISTIAN? WHEN TEXTS USE CHRISTIAN IDEAS

In selecting what we should read, most of us probably believe that Christian literature should be given priority. But what do we mean by "Christian literature"? Surely *Paradise Lost* is Christian literature, but what about *Hamlet?* Did Thomas Hardy, Oscar Wilde, Flannery O'Connor, C. S. Lewis and J. R. R. Tolkien all write Christian short stories? What makes a poem Christian or non-Christian?

We can attempt to define Christian literature in two ways: in terms of the religious belief of its author or in terms of the religious content of its text. Both methods of definition raise difficulties. Instead of labelling a work Christian or non-Christian, perhaps we should be more concerned to listen to what the text says and to evaluate how much of what it expresses is congruent with our belief.

Christian students in introductory literature courses often ask, "Was this author a Christian?" Sometimes this question reflects a partisan desire to enlist an acclaimed writer in the Christian camp: Hawthorne is such a good author, we think, he must be a Christian. More often the question comes out of insecurity: should I be agreeing with these views? Is this idea safe? Such questions are understandable, but to inquire about an author's faith is not often helpful.

The works in the traditional literary canon prior to the eighteenth century were written during a time when most writers thought of themselves as Christian and saw their life within a Christian framework. However, judging a particular author's religious commitment is very difficult, especially when we lack detailed biographical information. We will never know definitively in our earthly existence whether Shakespeare, for example, was a Christian. We can only say that he lived at a time when Christianity informed most people's lives and that his plays often express ideas compatible with Christianity. Does that make Shakespearean drama Christian?

Authors who wrote when there was no longer a Christian consensus are even more difficult to judge. Nathaniel Hawthorne said about his fellow novelist Herman Melville, "He can neither believe, nor be comfortable in his unbelief; and he is too honest and courageous not to try to do one or the other." Melville left no specific account in letters or journals about how he resolved his religious dilemma, and his biographers continue to debate whether he ever became reconciled to Christianity.

When we do not know the personal commitment of an author such as Melville, we may attempt to judge his religious convictions or label his work Christian or not on the basis of its content. But few literary texts will tell us if a writer knew Jesus as a personal savior. Instead, texts express ideas that may or may not be congruent with Christian belief and may or may not be exclusively Christian.

We can think of our faith as a beautiful musical composition, full of rich harmonies and intricate counterpoint; if we take out one or two parts, we may still recognize the melody even if the fullness has been diminished. Some works of literature are like this—thin versions of the complex Christian song. Other works may use some similar notes but add other, discordant passages. To evaluate what we read, we need to ask, "How well does this work resonate with my Christianity?"

A story about the value of self-sacrificing love may echo part of the Christian song, but it is not necessarily exclusively Christian. A Buddhist, a Unitarian, and a Shi'ite Muslim would probably all agree that to give up one's life to serve the greater good is an ethical act.

We may also want to call a work Christian when it includes specific Christian concepts, themes, stories, or allusions. Given the widespread influence of the Bible and Christianity on the development of Western culture, we will discover many such references. However, just because a text quotes the Bible or mentions a Christian idea, it does not necessarily sound the full Christian song or even a tune harmonious with Christianity.

A sympathetic treatment of Christian ideas in a text does not guarantee that the author is a Christian. Oscar Wilde, a nineteenth-century Irish writer, wrote a touching fairy tale, "The Selfish Giant," which suggests both that children should not be selfish (an idea congruent with Christianity) and that the unselfish Jesus died to redeem others (an idea exclusive to Christianity). However, Wilde's rather eccentric life did not conform to Christian principles. We only know that he wrote a story depicting Christian ideas in a sympathetic and approving manner.

Another way to see the limitations of judging an author by his or her text is to consider literature written by a professing Christian. Such texts do not necessarily contain specific Christian statements or doctrines. Christians believe that faith informs every aspect of life; it is not limited to a so-called "religious" realm. Consequently, the Christian convictions of a writer will inform everything she or he writes: a story about building a house will be just as Christian as a story about an answer to prayer.

A Christian poet I know often writes simple lyrics about his life and family, such as an account of a visit to a Southern barber shop or a celebration of his oldest daughter's fourteenth birthday. I wonder if someone who read these poems without knowing the author could tell that they were "Christian" poems. The texts reveal gentleness, humor, love, a sense of tradition, and a facility with language—but not explicit Christianity. My friend's faith governs all of his life, including his creative writing, and he honors God with these well-written lyrics. Even though his poems might not express exclusively Christian ideas, they embody a Christian understanding of life and language.

Using the content of a work, then, to decide whether it is Christian does not work very well, since some Christians may write works that are not uniquely Christian in their content, while some non-Christians write works that draw on Christian ideas or concur with Christian thought. To make judgments about an author's personal religious commitment does not help us to determine the value of a text. Our desire to label works of literature Christian or non-Christian, while common, is misdirected.

Nonetheless, Christian readers may encounter troublesome questions when reading texts that contain Christian references, texts written by professing Christians, and texts advocating ideas not compatible with Christianity. The rest of this chapter will examine these interpretive pitfalls and suggest some general principles to guide us through this rugged territory.

Reading Texts with Christian References

The Bible is one of the most important documents in the history of civilization, not only because of its status as holy inspired Scripture, but also because of its pervasive influence on Western thought. As the predominant world view for at least fourteen centuries, Christianity and its great central text played a major role in the formation of Western culture. Consequently, many literary texts, even those in our post-Christian era, frequently draw on the Bible and the Christian tradition.

Christian references can take many forms. Since the Bible, particularly the monumental King James Version, makes up the warp of our great cultural tapestry, most references are to biblical passages. Texts may include quotes or echoes of biblical language, as well as use biblical characters (Jonah, Peter), narratives (the Exodus), or image patterns (sins red as scarlet; manna, the living bread). Literary works may also refer to a distinctively Christian doctrine such as the Creation or the Atonement. Finally, Christian references may also include the particular traditions developed by the historical church such as the sacraments, Mariology, and major theologies (such as Calvinism or Lutheranism).

A culturally literate person today needs to be familiar with the Bible. While chairman of the National Endowment for the Humanities, William J. Bennett asked hundreds of educators along with the general public (in a newspaper column by George Will) to recommend ten books that all high school graduates should have read. His respondents cited four texts at least fifty percent of the time: Shakespeare's plays, the key American historical documents (the Constitution, Declaration of Independence, and Federalist Papers), *The Adventures of Huckleberry Finn*, and the Bible (Bennett, 10). Yet because so few people read and study the Bible carefully today, many schools have begun courses in "The Bible as Literature" or "The Bible in Literature," to give students the background necessary for understanding classic works of literature.

Biblically illiterate readers will never comprehend Milton's epic masterpiece, *Paradise Lost*, and will miss many of the key image patterns in William Faulkner's fiction. Biblically illiterate readers need aids like the lengthy footnote in the Norton edition of *Moby-Dick* explaining the opening line, "Call me Ishmael":

The biblical Ishmael was the son of Abraham by the bondservant Hagar, an Egyptian. Ishmael was disinherited and cast out in favor of his younger half-brother Isaac, Abraham's son by his wife Sarah. . . . The name was in common use to mean an exile or outcast. (12)

The effectiveness of such references depends on a shared body of knowledge, but increasingly our society no longer shares in the knowledge of the biblical tradition. We are impoverished readers because of this ignorance.

The Christian student who knows the Bible through years of hearing it read at home and at church, who analyzes it in Sunday school, Bible study, or Christian school, who meditates on it during personal and public devotions, and who repeats it during liturgical worship is at a distinct advantage when he or she reads texts with biblical references. The language and cadences of the Bible are part of our vocabulary; biblical narratives and images are as familiar to us as baseball, apple pie, and Chevrolet. If we have a good biblical and theological foundation, we will be better readers of many texts—more emotionally attuned to the resonances created by biblical associations, and more familiar with the biblical context when we interpret the new literary context.

However, sometimes we can be too sensitive. Some readers eagerly seize on every biblical reference and painstakingly search for a character who is thirty-two years old, or dies, or suffers, or has the initials J. C. We find Christ figures behind every tree and attempt to wring a Christian message out of every text, no matter how theologically dry. When Henry David Thoreau ends his account of "Spring" in *Walden* with the words "O Death, where was thy sting? O Grave, where was thy victory, then?" we conclude that he was a Christian. We make mountains out of molehills, distort connections, and conclude hastily and inaccurately.

Christian references in a text are important, but most often they are only part of a complex linguistic structure with many other kinds of references. Because we are more attuned to Christian references, we may overestimate their function in the text. A literary text employs Christian references for numerous reasons, and as we read, we must determine why these references are employed, and what kind of meaning they add to the text.

Texts That Focus on Christian Topics

Certain texts primarily feature Christian material. Some retell a biblical story or focus on a biblical character, as does, for example, Milton's verse narrative *Paradise Lost,* Robert Lowell's poem "King David Old," or Archibald Macleish's Pulitzer-winning drama *J.B.* Other texts may have a Christian as their central character or may focus on specific Christian traditions. For example, ever since David wrote Psalm 122 celebrating his joy in the day of worship, numerous poets have examined the tradition of Sabbath observance. (See George Herbert's "Sunday," Emily Dickinson's "Some keep the Sabbath going to Church," Philip Larkin's "Church-Going," and Louis MacNeice's "Sunday Morning," for a few very different examples.)

Although we may be pleased to find works based on Christian narratives, characters, or practices, we must not hastily conclude that they endorse or advocate Christian ideas. When an author structures a text around a biblical narrative or character, we must ask, "Does the text affirm the biblical text to be significant in Christian terms?" Donald Davie provides some excellent advice when he says that we need to consider if a text embodies "the doctrinal implications of the story" (xxi).

A play about King David's affair with Bathsheba that focuses on the romantic human emotions of the two lovers without presenting the sinfulness of the act or their need for repentance does not affirm Christianity. The doctrinal implications of sin are necessary notes for the full song. However, a text that omits doctrinal implications is not necessarily denying Christianity or criticizing its values.

Louis MacNeice's poem "Sunday Morning," for example, uses the Christian concept of Sunday as a device to describe a new secular religion. The poem depicts common Sunday morning activities: someone is practicing scales, and "Man's heart expands to tinker with his car." After revving up the engine, the man drives so fast that he makes the day "a small eternity" until the church bells call him back to reality, "the weekday time. Which deadens and endures." While describing the typical contemporary practice of Sunday leisure, the poem suggests through its diction ("heart expands") and imagery (eternity, church bells) that our age has developed new objects of worship. Because its focus is the secular Sabbath, the poem neither affirms nor denies the value of Christian ideas about Sabbath observance.

As a major shaping force in our culture, the Christian tradition contributes many items to the storehouse of literary devices from which an author draws. Christian readers may more easily recognize elements of this tradition than others, but we must exercise care in reading texts that focus on biblical narratives or Christian traditions. We must neither embrace these works too quickly as endorsing Christian ideas nor spurn them too rashly as rejecting Christian values.

Texts That Include Biblical Allusions

Some texts focus on Christian topics, but the more common kind of Christian textual references come in the form of subtle allusions to the Bible. An *allusion* is a figure of speech that refers to a literary or historical person, place, or event. If you say, "My father is a Goliath of a man," you refer to the biblical character of Goliath in order to explain something about your father.

The context of the allusion determines its function. If you continue by describing your father's size 12 shoe and claim that your mother looks like Thumbelina next to him, the allusion works differently from the way it would if you went on to call him an unbelieving Philistine who needs a David in his life. In the first case, the allusion evokes Goliath's immense size; in the second, his symbolic stature as a foe to true faith.

Biblical allusions may come individually or in organized patterns like those of David, Goliath, and the Philistines. Individual allusions usually add a single resonance or quality, such as Goliath's size, to the literary text, but patterns of allusion are more complex, introducing another narrative against which to judge the literary narrative. By alluding to the biblical narrative of David and Goliath, you imply your father's resistance to Christianity, your awe of his authoritative position, and your longing for a small event to bring down his pride.

This kind of organized series of biblical allusions is often called *typology,* and is based on the theological practice of reading certain events and characters in the Old Testament as "types" foreshadowing events and characters in the New Testament. When Jacob is sold into captivity by his jealous brothers, he foreshadows Jesus' betrayal into the hands of Pilate by his own people and so is a type of Christ. In literary typology, the pattern of allusions suggests a biblical story against which the textual account may be seen.

Biblical allusions add meaning to a text through either their similarity or their contrast. On the one hand, the biblical meaning may enlarge or enhance the literary text. So, when you call your father a Goliath in our first example, you suggest his strength and size by associating him with the biblical giant. The allusion works by means of similarity.

On the other hand, allusions can also undercut a textual subject by displaying a marked difference between the subject and the allusion. In T. S. Eliot's "The Love Song of J. Alfred Prufrock," the narrator laments, "Though I have seen my head (grown slightly bald) brought in upon a platter, / I am no prophet—and here's no great matter." The allusion contrasts the outspoken nature of the biblical prophet to the timidity of Prufrock, who is only an ironic John the Baptist.

Several principles should guide the reading of biblical allusions. First, we must decide if the allusion is isolated or if it forms part of a pattern. Single allusions should not be read typologically as if they evoked all the attributes or events of the reference but should be considered in light of the context of the surrounding text. When you call your father a Goliath in the context of his shoe size and your mother's petite figure, you narrow the allusiveness of your reference to Goliath's physical appearance and do not include his moral nature or spiritual significance.

Second, a series of allusions needs to be internally consistent before it becomes typology. Describing your mother as Sarah, your father as Isaac, and yourself as David does not set up a logical pattern the way describing your mother as Sarah, your father as Abraham, and yourself as Isaac does.

Third, with typological allusion we must be careful to submit the biblical narrative to the context of the literary work and not vice versa. We must not distort the literary work in an attempt to make it follow the biblical story in every detail. As English professor John H. Timmerman cautions, the patterns of typology "are themes *against which* we observe the primary action of the work. They are not the determining action itself, but the imaginative context, the frame for consideration of the action" (27). The pattern of allusion evokes a comparison only as an addition to the primary meaning of the text.

Finally, using the context of the literary work and our knowledge of its biblical allusions, we must decide what kind of meaning—similarity or ironic contrast—the allusions add to the text.

Besides contributing to the meaning of the literary text, biblical allusions occasionally also comment on the original text, the Bible. Speaking about allusions in general, Professor Robert Weisbuch distinguishes between *friendly* and *competitive* allusions:

> an allusion may be friendly, with the intent of clarifying or broadening something in the present text by invoking an earlier text, with no effect of derogating that source; or an allusion may be competitive and parodic, employing the words of an earlier text to challenge them by a ridiculing alteration or by the changed context of the surroundings in the new text. (xix)

In Weisbuch's terms, a friendly allusion accepts the tradition of the Bible as a useful source without necessarily affirming its truth, but a competitive allusion challenges the biblical tradition and its values.

Competitive allusion works in Tennessee Williams's *The Glass Menagerie* to demonstrate the deficiencies of Christianity. In this play, Amanda dreams of the day that her crippled daughter Laura will receive a gentleman caller. When Laura's brother Tom finally convinces Jim O'Connor, one of his coworkers, to call on her, the word "Annunciation" appears on a screen. Jim is an ordinary young man who believes in self-improvement, technological progress, and romantic love. Laura is attracted to him, but when Jim admits that he is engaged to another girl, she is crushed.

Tom narrates the play and tells us in the opening scene that Jim symbolizes "the long delayed but always expected something that we live for." The biblical echoes and allusions establish Jim O'Connor as a type of savior; however, the primary action of the play demonstrates how he embodies a futile salvation offered by the church, by romantic love, and by the gospel of success. In this case, the allusions challenge the biblical text by presenting a parody of its values and associating it with other futile attempts to give meaning to life.

Texts with Christ Figures and Christian Characters

Jim O'Connor represents one of the most commonly occurring yet most frequently misunderstood Christian references: the Christ figure. The character and story of Christ can provide the central focus for a text, as in Jim Bishop's novel *The Day Christ Died,* but most frequently references to Christ in literary texts are allusions, either in individual passages or in organized patterns. Just as with other biblical allusions, we need to judge the context in which the reference appears, whether the allusion evokes similarity or contrast, and if the reference is friendly or competitive. References to Christ do not all function in the same way, and we often read them too simplistically.

One of the most common misreadings of allusions to Christ is to interpret a character as a Christ figure based on only one or two isolated allusions. For example, when Herman Melville's *Billy Budd* says that the sergeant-at-arms Claggart looks "like the man of sorrows," we should not conclude that Claggart is a type of Christ in his moral character or actions. The plot of the story, the narrator's comments, and the other image patterns associating him with a snake or scorpion make it clear that Claggart is evil. The allusion merely suggests the depth and agony of Claggart's occasional moments of sorrow.

If a coherent pattern of allusion suggests a character is a type of Christ, the typology can function either to elevate the character by means of the similarity or to deflate the character because of the ironic contrast. Far too often we accept Christ figures in texts as exemplary because we have not noticed the irony invoked by the juxtaposition of the biblical allusions to the primary action of the text.

The allusions to Captain Ahab as a Christ figure in Herman Melville's *Moby-Dick* work in an ironic way. The legends about Ahab include the story that he lay as though dead for three days after the great white whale took off his leg; he appears "with a crucifixion in his face" and "wakes with his own bloody nails in his palms" (111,

174). But Ahab is not a Christ-like figure. Judging these allusions against the primary action of *Moby-Dick,* we see Ahab as an ironic Christ who inhumanely sacrifices the lives of his crew during the course of his insane pursuit of the white whale.

Probably the most difficult conclusion to draw about Christ figures is whether the allusions are friendly or competitive. Authors may use Christ imagery out of respect because they think Jesus provides an admirable example. However, they may see Jesus either as Christ, the Son of the living God and the Savior of human beings, or as a good man and an ethical teacher. The vague nature of allusions and their secondary role in the text means that we may not be able to deduce from them that the text demonstrates the doctrinal implications of Christ's life.

Similarly, when a text employs Christ imagery to undercut an inadequate character, we may wonder whether this irony is double-sided and also reflects discredit upon the true Christ. Ironic Christ figures might challenge the value of Christianity, as the rendition of Jim O'Connor in *The Glass Menagerie* does. However, ironic allusions may be more neutral and employ the biblical text only to demonstrate the flaws of the literary character. Melville's rendition of Ahab does not seem to me to be commenting on the failure of Christianity so much as on the failure of the monomaniacal captain. Again, we must examine the primary narrative carefully to determine whether the author criticizes the Christian system of belief through the ironic Christ figure.

Some texts may depict a special kind of Christ figure in a character who is a believer or member of the clergy. Most of us have no trouble interpreting strong Christian characters such as the hero of *Pilgrim's Progress* or Alyosha in Fyodor Dostoyevsky's *The Brothers Karamazov.* But texts that show Christians in a negative light are more troublesome. They may be making comments either on the inadequacies of Christianity or on the inadequacies of some human embodiments of Christianity. In *The Adventures of Huckleberry Finn,* when Mark Twain satirizes both Tom Sawyer's romantic fantasies and Miss

Watson's religion as impractical, he seems to criticize Christianity as a system of belief.

But the presence of an unsympathetic Christian character does not necessarily mean that a text is opposed to Christian thought. For example, the hypocritical excesses of the clergyman Mr. Brocklehurst in *Jane Eyre*, who makes his orphan wards dress in paper-thin gowns and cuts off their curls while his sisters enjoy elaborate dresses and hairstyles, stem more from his class snobbery than his religious beliefs. We must determine whether the failures of the Christian character stem from Christian thought or from personal flaws before we can decide if the text criticizes Christianity.

Reading texts with Christian references, then, is a tricky business. In some important respects we may find ourselves more prepared than other readers, but we also come with certain prejudices of which we must be aware. Texts that focus on Christian topics, or include biblical references or Christ figures, require careful interpretation, not rash conclusions.

Reading Texts Written by Christians

Although we cannot judge an author's personal commitment to Christ by means of his or her literary efforts, often we know that certain authors are Christians because they have openly professed their faith. John Donne, George Herbert, and John Milton were vocal Christians; C. S. Lewis, J. R. R. Tolkien, and Dorothy L. Sayers all made a point of discussing their religious beliefs and how those beliefs affected their writing. When we read the work of contemporary authors such as Frederick Buechner, Sietze Buning, John Leax, Madeleine L'Engle, James Schaap, Virginia Stem Owens, Walker Percy, Walter Wangerin, and Rudy Wiebe, we know that these authors confess Christian belief. How does this knowledge affect our reading of their texts?

At first we may think that they would be easier to read. After all, we are going to agree with these authors, and surely we will enjoy their work. However, in actuality, the particular content and technical qualities of such texts must be analyzed with as much care as we would give any text.

Even if the author is a Christian, we might still disagree with his or her ideas since the Christian community itself has a plurality of opinions. Depending on your own theological background, you may find points where you want to refine or alter or even reject L'Engle's Episcopalian views, Schaap's Reformed perspectives, or Percy's Catholic outlook.

We also should remember that the Christian vision unfolds gradually. Guided by the authority of the Scriptures and the leadership of the church, we now understand Christianity in a different way than would a person living in Chaucer's England or in antebellum Georgia. The ideas expressed in the writing of a medieval Christian or a slave-owning Bible believer will undoubtedly be very different from our own beliefs. Knowing that the author is a Christian does not necessarily imply that we will agree with everything the text says.

Works written by Christians, then, need the same kind of careful analysis as other texts. The next three chapters will discuss some of these ways to evaluate a text. However, literature written by Christians also raises some unique questions. What kind of textual strategies does a contemporary Christian employ when writing in a post-Christian world? Why do some Christians write fantasies and others prefer realistic works? Is there such a thing as a Christian style of writing? In many ways, knowing that the author of a work is a Christian only complicates the reading process, but it makes it more exciting as well.

Reading Texts Written by Non-Christians

To confine our reading to literature written by professed Christians would significantly limit our understanding, cultivation, and enjoyment of God's creation. All of the benefits of reading discussed in the first part of this book may derive equally from works written by Christians and non-Christians. Interpretation, metaphor, and narrative inform our lives, and as we read we become more skilled interpreters and analysts. Reading books helps us serve God in developing his world as we explore new experiences and ideas. Reading allows us to identify and celebrate beauty and truth. Along with Salieri in the play *Amadeus*, we may wonder why God gave great artistic gifts to unworthy vessels, but like the rain, the gift to construct good texts and to wield textual power falls on the just and the unjust alike.

Because, as St. Ambrose stated, "all truth is God's truth," works of literature that do not articulate specific Christian ideas can express ideas that are congruent with our Christianity. The plays of Shakespeare seldom reveal explicit Christian doctrines but nonetheless powerfully convey important truths about human interactions in their narratives. We can learn much about love from *Romeo and Juliet*, about revenge from *Macbeth*, and about forgiveness from *King Lear*. To read such works allows us to grow as Christians.

Often we will agree with and learn from part of a poem or story but disagree with other parts. A work might strike certain notes that resonate with Christianity, but also sound some discordant notes. The American transcendentalists Ralph Waldo Emerson and Henry David Thoreau remind us that we are often too attached to our earthly belongings at the cost of our spiritual growth, but we cannot agree with their pantheism and disregard for humanity's sinful nature. But even though we recognize some errors in *Walden* or "Nature," we can profit from reading these works.

Texts by non-Christian authors help us to conceive of some of our non-Christian neighbors' ideas about life. This is especially true of writing from the nineteenth and twentieth century, when the Christian world view lost its authoritative position, and people began looking for alternative ways to make life meaningful. We can learn much from the works of the nineteenth-century English and American romantics; the turn-of-the-century realists, naturalists, and determinists; the mid-twentieth-century existentialists; and our contemporary parodic metafictionalists. All these writers explore new ways to interpret life and employ new kinds of metaphor and narrative.

The work of an author such as Ernest Hemingway embodies common cultural ideas about love, war, human worth, and mortality that we not only need to know intellectually but also need to understand in a deeper way in order to minister effectively to our neighbors. Before we can reach others, we must understand what they are feeling and why they are feeling that way.

Hemingway's short stories and novels express the frustration many people feel as they attempt to find meaning and happiness through living on the edge of disaster—whether the subject is big-game hunting, bullfighting, or the battlefield. Our contemporaries similarly gamble with drugs, sex, and AIDS. Hemingway's works always sadden me, but they also help me to understand many of my non-Christian friends.

As we read works written by non-Christians, then, we can learn to know ourselves and our society better. We attempt to identify the truths with which we agree and the false notes we must reject. We enjoy literary techniques, savor magnificent workmanship, and rejoice in the beauty of the text. The profusion of literary texts in our world represent the variety of ways, both good and flawed, that human beings have attempted to develop God's creation and to participate in his world, whether conscious of his hand or ignorant of the true King.

Chapter 11

EVALUATING LITERATURE: THE GOOD, THE BAD, AND THE UGLY

Once there was a great king who wore a huge crown of gold encrusted with diamonds and emeralds. This king was a mighty warrior and an even mightier lover, for he had many wives and mistresses who bore him numerous children. His sons grew strong and handsome; his daughters were spirited and beautiful.

Over the course of time the King's oldest son, Arn, developed a passion for one of his half-sisters, a slender girl named Tara, who wore the embroidered robes that indicated she was still a virgin. Obsessed with her beauty and purity, Arn tossed and turned at night, fantasizing about having sex with her. He lost his appetite, and dark shadows encircled his eyes.

Finally, his friend Jones, a shrewd and cunning man, asked, "Why do you, the King's son, look so haggard morning after morning? Won't you tell me?"

Arn answered, "I'm in love with Tara, my brother's sister. What can I do? I can't stop thinking about her."

Jones reflected for a minute, and then said, "Here's how you can fulfill your desire. Go to bed and pretend to be sick. You certainly look bad enough. Your father will come to visit you, and when he asks if he can do anything for you, ask him to have Tara bring you some of her special honey bread."

Arn followed Jones's advice. The King visited him and hearing his request, immediately sent for Tara, who came and began preparing the bread. But when she brought a loaf to Arn, he refused to eat.

"Send everyone out of here," Arn ordered. So his friends, his servants, and even his doctor departed. Jones was the last to leave, and as he closed the door, he gave Arn a knowing look.

"Now bring the bread here," Arn told his sister. When she came close to him, he grabbed her arm and pulled her down next to him. "Come to bed with me," he whispered.

Frightened and alarmed, Tara struggled to break free. "Don't," she cried. "Don't force me. Don't do this wicked thing."

Arn paid no attention. She then attempted to reason with him: "Think of me. I would be disgraced. And what about you? You'd be known as the wickedest fool in the kingdom. Talk to the King; maybe he could arrange for us to be married."

But Arn was caught up in his physical feelings, and he refused to listen. Using his strength to overpower her, he raped his sister.

As soon as his lust was satisfied, Arn's obsession turned to hate. "Get up and get out of here," he ordered.

"No," she said. "Sending me away would be even more wrong than what you have already done to me."

But his hate was now as strong as his love had been before. He called his servant and said crudely, "Get this woman out of here and bolt the door after her." So the servant roughly turned out the weeping Tara.

After putting ashes on her head, Tara ripped her embroidered robe, for she no longer was a virgin. Covering her shamed face with her hands, she left Arn's house, weeping aloud as she went through the city, a desolate woman.

When the King heard all of this, he was furious.

Not a very pleasant tale, is it? In fact, the story of Arn and Tara is deeply upsetting in its account of warped human emotion and physical abuse. Texts such as this pose difficulties for us as we decide what we should read. If we are to follow Paul's advice in Philippians to think on true, noble, right, pure, lovely, and admirable things, how can we read works that depict false, dishonorable, wrong, corrupt, ugly, and despicable things?

The story of Tara's rape is one of lust, deception, scheming, and brutality. It tells of misplaced physical drives, of a woman treated like an object, of false friends, and of an ineffective parent. It is a story full of immorality. It is also a biblical story about the problems in King David's family (2 Samuel 13).

The Bible is full of such stories. It paints a complete picture of the variety of sins that human beings are capable of committing. Murder, blasphemy, sexual perversion, torture, idol worship, child sacrifice, slavery, prostitution, dehumanization, exploitation of the poor, pride, envy, and gluttony—the Bible shows it all, often in graphic detail.

Yet we all believe that we should read the Bible. We know that the Bible's accounts of human sin are different from the pornographic renditions of similar acts found in the reading material of an adult book store. But we must sort through the differences carefully in order to determine how to distinguish the good from the bad, and how to evaluate literature as Christians.

Such evaluation should go beyond awareness of a text's subject matter and language to include scrutiny of its treatment of the subject, its moral and ethical perspectives, its vision of life, its context within the larger framework of literature, and its artistic achievement. Issues of morality for the Christian are far more complex than the question of whether a work should be labelled "dirty" because it includes a profane word or depicts an act of adultery.

Reading and Morality

A discussion of morality and literature would be pointless to some twentieth-century readers, who believe that texts are amoral (neither moral nor immoral) and that a text should only be judged on artistic grounds. The novelist and critic William H. Gass, for example, thinks that works of literature are just beautiful objects. He claims, "Artistic quality depends upon a work's . . . structure and its style, and not upon the morality it is presumed to recommend" ("Goodness," 42). Gass is far more interested in how a text is put together than in what it actually says. He believes that reading is a process of contemplation, appreciation, and "disinterested affection" ("Goodness," 44).

Some Christian readers have felt that they could read literature as Gass does, at first examining only the style and structure, and then finishing their criticism with a Christian response to the content of the work. The Christian poet and critic T. S. Eliot, for example, suggests that "literary criticism should be completed by criticism from a definite ethical and theological standpoint" (21). Eliot sees reading as involving two discrete steps: an objective analysis of artistic qualities followed by a subjective evaluation. But this kind of approach is impossible; we are always interested and prejudiced readers.

Reading can never be neatly divided into two objective and subjective steps. What a text says cannot be easily separated from how it is written. Form and content are interdependent parts of the total meaning of a text, and our analysis and evaluation will encompass both. Also, some kind of value system will inform all our reactions, and if we do not consciously engage Christian values throughout our reading, we will inevitably use some other standard of measurement.

Those Christians who believe they can objectively discuss the aesthetic or artistic qualities of a work of literature are employing the values of "formalist" (concerned with form) criticism. The belief that one can discuss a poem's ambiguities, tensions, and paradoxes in an objective, scientific manner is itself a value-judgment, an assumption that structure is more important than content, or "that art is more important than people," as the critic Wayne Booth phrases it (49).

Many contemporary readers have come to realize that all criticism is somehow informed by the critic's own values. Instead of allowing our culture to form our position entirely, Christians should consciously attempt to employ biblically-grounded values throughout the entire reading process. We must practice a fully integrated evaluation of literature instead of the two-step approach. Biblical standards of language, of personhood, of right and wrong, of interpretation, and of beauty must shape our evaluation of all works of literature.

Textual Power

God has given us the ability to use written language that is meaningful and that helps us to interact with others and our world. Consequently, texts can communicate ideas and attitudes through their formal design and intellectual content. Such communicative ability constitutes a powerful force, and this textual power can be abused. One such abuse occurs when we become desensitized to the power that language, metaphors, and narratives can wield.

When a Soviet colonel signs a death warrant for an Afghan rebel, the power of his written text is readily apparent. We must not forget that the texts of the newspapers and magazines around us are just as powerful, even if they are more subtle. They attempt to mold our thoughts and desires: "Buy me!" "Drink me, and women will be attracted to you!" "Wear me, and men will think you are sexy!" "Live this way, use this product, and you will be happy!"

The texts that have perhaps the greatest influence on us are those with which we spend the most amount of time: television shows, movies, and popular literature. These texts have such influence because we seldom think about them carefully. As we use such works for entertainment and relaxation, they convey messages and values that we absorb and that may unconsciously influence us.

Robert Scholes clearly summarizes the importance of evaluating what we read:

that is the whole function of criticism. It is a way of discovering how to choose, how to take some measure of responsibility for ourselves and for our world. Criticism is our last best chance to loosen the bonds of the textual powers in which we find ourselves enmeshed. (75)

Readers concerned about the moral consequences of reading attempt to bring textual power under control and to use it wisely to better serve God and their neighbors. They recognize the pervasive and persuasive nature of textual communication and attempt to be careful readers. Unlike Gass, Christian readers cannot agree that the goodness of a text depends only on its artistic achievements. We also must demand that it use textual power wisely to tell the truth about people and the world in ways that are helpful rather than harmful.

In our evaluation, then, we must consider the values that a work of literature expresses. A work that upholds an immoral perspective is artistically flawed. As Booth asserts, "the quality of an artwork's ideology [ideas or opinions] affects its quality *as art*" (49).

In a concern to be thoroughly Christian readers, though, we must be careful not to label works simply "sound" or "unsound," Christian or non-Christian. Literary works are complex structures that communicate a variety of concepts simultaneously. We should not take a story such as Hawthorne's *The Scarlet Letter*, conclude that its moral is, "thou shalt not commit adultery," and stamp it with a Christian seal of approval. A one-sentence summary can never capture the full meaning of a work; when we read, the structure of a story explores multiple directions of thought and opens up numerous possibilities.

Booth provides a helpful way to think about the dangers of a too-simple moral criticism:

Don't reduce fictions . . . to a simple conflict of doctrines or dogmas. Don't assume that an idea expressed in a great complex imaginative work is exactly the same as the 'same' idea when it is extracted and restated in your critical work. Art can do what no other human activity can do, and you will not find freedom of interpretation by a simple rejection of what seemed to be said by it. (70)

Instead, we must explore the world and ideas of the text in detail, finding both its strengths and its weaknesses, determining the extent of its congruence with our own values, and appreciating the new avenues of thought that it opens up for us.

Judging Obscenity

In literature, as in all human activity, we find abundant evidence of our fallen human nature; but the fact that a work of literature shows us something sinful does not automatically mean that we should condemn it as obscene. Wise Christian readers need to consider the text's *purpose* and *point of view* in their evaluation. In other words, we must decide what kind of action the text is encouraging us to take.

The Bible talks about human corruption in order to teach us important lessons about our nature and our need for salvation. Its purpose for depicting immorality is to provide us with moral and spiritual insights. In order to convince us of our sin and our need for grace, God gives not only general guidelines like the Ten Commandments but also vivid and memorable examples of the evil of humanity. God's prohibition against sexual immorality is more meaningful when we see the anguish of David's brutalized daughter.

Truly obscene literature, on the other hand, depicts human sin in order to encourage its practice. The most obvious example of this kind of obscenity is pornography, which explicitly describes physical acts in order to stimulate the reader sexually. Pornography thus often depicts women merely as degraded sexual objects. We can also find instances of what I would call social or ethical pornography: texts that encourage readers to treat people with a different skin color as inferior or that recommend greed and dishonesty as justifiable ways to achieve success.

Rather than simply ask if a work depicts sin, we should determine its point of view on that sin. Does it affirm and encourage the exploitation of the poor, or is it showing such exploitation to point to the moral failure of companies that fail to treat their Third World workers justly? Does it include obscene and profane language gratuitously (without purpose), or does that language function to reveal something about the characters or setting?

A story that contains an act of adultery is not necessarily immoral or obscene. If the perspective of the story implies that adultery is an acceptable social practice that harms no one, the story advocates an immoral position with which we would disagree. But other stories may contain different points of view. David's affair with Bathsheba in 2 Sam. 11–12 has disastrous results; the context of the entire story shows how God revealed the King's sin through the prophet Nathan and punished the evil that David had done.

The short stories of the contemporary writer John Updike are full of disillusioned people who engage in meaningless acts of adultery in an effort to find happiness in the modern world. Their adultery is not affirmed, nor even shown in a positive light. Instead, Updike's work reveals the hopelessness of adultery to be one of the truths of suburban life.

In order to determine the purpose and point of view of the text, we must learn how to read carefully and to analyze the work as a whole. The Catholic writer Flannery O'Connor feels that many Christian readers "are overconscious of what they consider to be obscenity in modern fiction for the very simple reason that in reading a book, they have nothing else to look for" (188). Overly sensitive readers are often ignorant readers: "They are totally unconscious of the design, the tone, the intention, the meaning, or even the truth of what they have in hand. They don't see the book in a perspective that would reduce every part of it to its proper place in the whole" (188).

The reader is the final arbiter of a text's morality. We can always distort the text's point of view, take part of it out of context, or use the words for a different purpose. A corrupt reader could easily read the story found in 2 Samuel 13 as a guide to a successful seduction rather than as a horrifying account of human failure. Part of our responsibility as readers, then, is to deal with texts fairly, considering the author's intentions and the meaning of the work as a whole.

Reading well requires careful judgment and sharp interpretive skills. Some works, particularly those including sexual material, demand more emotional and intellectual maturity. Few children's Bible storybooks give a detailed account of David and Bathsheba or include the story of the incestuous rape of David's daughter. That's because children are not sophisticated enough as readers to be able to understand the purpose of such stories. In our own lives, we must use wisdom and the guidance of others more knowledgeable than ourselves to decide when we are capable of reading works with especially troubling content.

Dangerous Immorality

If we agree that moral issues are vitally important as we read, that reading has meaning and consequences, we also must agree that moral issues encompass more than profanity and sexual explicitness. Sometimes we get so concerned with offensive language or sex that we overlook many other kinds of depictions of sin that may prove far more tempting and harmful for us to read.

If we think about the immoral acts depicted in literature that pose the most temptation to us, are profanity and sexual sin really the most dangerous? Aren't we far more likely to be influenced by our society's ideals of self-centeredness; the glorification of alcoholic or drug-induced irrationality; the importance of money, clothing, and physical possessions; the need to be beautiful and have a perfect body; or the assumption that cheating and manipulation are acceptable practices?

Consider the values displayed in best-selling works that proclaim themselves in their ads in *The New York Times Book Review:* "a romp rife with drugs . . . greed and power, all delivered at a breathless pace"; "a rich and stylish tale of glamour, decadence, and revenge in America's high-stakes playground."

Some of the most dangerous immorality in texts today has nothing to do with sex or profanity. It lies instead in the acceptance of materialism, the encouragement of egotism, and the glorification of violence. Our attitudes can be seriously corrupted by the uncritical acceptance of a text that implies that a woman will never be completely fulfilled unless she has a man, or that true masculinity involves mowing down thousands of Asian people with a machine gun. A text containing profanity that prompts us to consider the sanctity of life, or a text with an explicit sexual encounter that shows the pain caused by using people as objects may be much more admirable, much less profane.

Good Morals and Bad Style

Gass's insistence that literature be judged by its artistic qualities is not all wrong. But a Christian reader understands the connection between beauty and truth and realizes that complete beauty includes truth. Reading is a moral act, not only because texts have meaning and power, but because our delight in good workmanship is part of our proper response to God. We appreciate the talents that God has given to others; we delight in the works of beauty that human beings have been able to craft because they live in God's world and have been given gifts by their creator.

When we understand the meaningfulness of literature in this light, our requirements for good literature will include craftsmanship as well as morality. A poem full of poor word choices, dull metaphors, and contorted syntax struggling to achieve a rhyme does not magnify the Lord, even if its subject is the resurrection. An excellently crafted poem celebrating the beauty of a rose is far superior, even if it never mentions God. A story with stilted dialogue, unbelievable characters, and boring language is not good, even if it concludes with a conversion. A Christian message or moral cannot redeem a text marred by shoddy workmanship.

Flannery O'Connor insists, "Poorly written novels—no matter how pious and edifying the behavior of the characters—are not good in themselves and are therefore not really edifying" (174). But what about those people who were converted or grew spiritually by reading poorly written texts? O'Connor answers such objections: "We have plenty of examples in this world of poor things being used for good purposes. God can make any indifferent thing, as well as evil itself, an instrument for good; but I submit that to do this is the business of God and not of any human being" (174).

A few years ago a Christian publisher sent a writer-friend of mine guidelines for a new series of Christian romance novels. My friend was appalled to receive detailed instructions on how to write such a book, including instructions on when the heroine should finally agree to kiss the hero and when the conversion was to take place. Writing in *Newsweek*, Kenneth L. Woodward describes the typical plot of these "inspirational romances": "suave but secular Lotharios are forever tempting young Christian maidens—bodies tremble and lips part—but eventually the heroine enters the promised land of Christian marriage" (69).

This kind of writing purports to be morally righteous, and readers may be thankful for its lack of profanity and chaste bedroom scenes, but its mechanical structure reflects its moral shallowness. It follows rote formulas and holds the reader's interest with titillating fantasy, rather than with realism. It demeans faith and sexuality when it makes the woman's body a prize that the hero wins for becoming Christian. Would God look at a book like this and declare that it was "good"? Such works of literature are only apparently pious. If we look closer, we may decide that they are actually immoral. The morality of art as a Christian understands it includes artistic quality.

Inspired by our knowledge of God and the consequences stemming from the influential power of literature, Christian readers acknowledge that reading is a moral act. In order to be responsible readers, we must judge literature carefully. A responsible reader will 1) grant that values always inform the act of reading, 2) attempt to put Christian values to work in his or her reading, 3) consider the purpose and point of view of the text, and 4) realize that texts may be immoral in other ways than by using profanity and sexual explicitness.

Chapter 12

HOW LITERARY FORMS CREATE MEANING

Do you remember eating alphabet soup as a child? Nothing was more fun than to dig around in the bowl for the noodle-letters so you could spell "pig" or "dog" on your spoon. Even more fun was turning to your sister and flourishing the word as somehow indicative of her personality. In a very basic way, the alphabet soup game reflects our natural attraction to structure. Given a chaotic glob of noodles, we attempt to form them into a meaningful order.

An author is like a child with alphabet soup. The huge soup bowl of the world is full of words, characters, situations, images, and ideas. In writing a work of literature, the author takes these available materials and somehow puts them into a meaningful form. Just as letters combine to form words, so groups of words can be ordered in such a way as to produce an essay, a play, or a poem. As authors work with the material in God's world, they obey God's commands to develop his creation and to employ their talents meaningfully.

Without structure and forms, texts would have no meaning. If you found the letters *g, o,* and *d* in your soup and arranged them as *ogd,* your flourished spoon would not say anything to your sister. And if you put the letters together to read *god,* you would communicate something very different from *dog.*

Sometimes students become impatient with their literature teachers' apparent obsession with meter and rhyme, imagery and points of view, protagonists and antagonists. What do all those things have to do with reading? they wonder. Why can't we just read the story or poem and see what it says?

The alphabet soup analogy suggests that what the story or poem says is in fact determined, in part, by the ways its author has chosen to order language and experience. For example, if you have three events that could be part of a story, such as a marriage, a journey, and a death, the order in which these events occur determines the kind of story that you tell. A story arranged "death, journey, marriage" is very different from a story of "marriage, journey, death." The way that the elements of literature—ranging from individual words to larger plot actions or image patterns—are put into a certain form produces the meaning of a particular work. Consequently, by learning how to apprehend and interpret the different structures of a text, we become better readers and enhance our reading experience.

Generic Forms

One of the most common ways to discuss the structure of a literary work is to examine its *genre*. Simply defined, genres are the different categories into which literary works are grouped according to the form they take. For example, a work of literature divided into numerous short lines centered on a page is obviously a poem. While the formation of the lines is the most recognizable feature, poems often have other structuring devices such as meter and rhyme. Every genre has its own recognizable formal devices, which are called *conventions*.

Often literature courses and textbooks focus on the three most common genres: fiction, poetry, and drama. But essays, diaries, histories, autobiographies, letters, and criticism are also important literary genres. If we think that literature is only fiction, poetry, or drama, we will overlook many great works such as Donne's sermons, Milton's essays, Boswell's *Life of Johnson*, Mary Rowlandson's account of her captivity by American Indians, Ralph Waldo Emerson's journals, and Frederick Douglass's autobiography. Courses that focus only on fiction, poetry, and drama deliberately narrow their coverage, most likely in order to teach the specific skills needed to read the most frequently appearing genres.

Over the years, ideas about genres have changed significantly. Ancient classical writers first divided literature into tragedy, comedy, epic, satire, lyric, and pastoral. These categories indicated the content of the work as well as the form; a tragedy, for example, would have a certain kind of plot and would be a play. Eighteenth- and nineteenth-century writers developed the new forms of the novel, personal essay, and philosophical poem. New genres of the twentieth century include screenplays, television scripts, and music videos.

Until the end of the eighteenth century, most critics believed that genres constituted absolutely fixed forms with particular rules governing style, subject matter, and structure. These critics evaluated a work in terms of how well it followed the rules of its genre. A good example of prescriptive reading by genre is the common eighteenth-century criticism (and sometimes revision) of Shakespeare for his failure to follow the rule of unities, which held that plays should be limited to one setting, to a 24-hour time period, and to one kind of plot.

Prescriptive critics also believed that some genres were better than others. Epic and tragedy were the greatest forms; lyric and pastoral were less important. Such strict rules disappeared in the nineteenth century as new forms evolved and the novel and the lyric poem became the preferred genres. Readers then began judging all genres by more general criteria, including expressiveness, seriousness, and use of organic, or naturally evolving, form.

We now can see that new forms emerge because authors constantly change and adapt formal conventions. Genres are constantly evolving. Some become more specialized. For example, the novel has developed into many *subgenres*, including the detective novel, the historical novel, and the romantic novel. Other genres become so general that they represent a perspective rather than a specific form, such as when *tragedy* became the *tragic vision* that we can find in poems and novels as well as in plays.

Genres today for the most part are no longer prescriptive—representing absolute rules and hierarchies, but instead are descriptive—constituting loosely defined categories. However, genre plays an important role both in structuring texts and in suggesting how we should read them. In the following pages we will see how the formal aspects of a work affect our reading of its content, add rational and emotional meaning to the text, and imply a philosophical position.

How Form Affects Content

Genres work most simply by putting the language of the work into a context that helps us to know how to read it. The genre of the work tells us what conventions the author will use and so suggests to us what *interpretive conventions* we should use. When we read a play, we don't expect Shakespeare to talk directly to us. We do expect extensive dialogue. We know we must base our opinion of King Lear on what the character says and does rather than on what the author says about him. Similarly, we read a poem using a different set of interpretive conventions than if we were reading a novel. We don't necessarily expect a plot or a set of characters in a poem; we do expect a single poetic voice.

In order to see more clearly how genre guides our reading, consider a hypothetical poet who wishes to comment on the continued international arms buildup, the threat of nuclear war, and the numerous armed conflicts raging in today's world. She entitles her work, "Moribund," which means both "at the point of death, about to die" and "approaching an end, obsolescent." The poem contains the exact words of a dictionary entry for *peace* arranged in poetic lines. The first stanza reads:

> Moribund
> (pes) *n.* 1. The absence
> of war or other hostilities. 2. An agreement
> or treaty to end
> hostilities:
> *the Peace of Westphalia.*
> 3. Freedom
> from quarrels and disagreement.

Although these words are taken directly from *The American Heritage Dictionary,* in this context they are poetry.

Given two different contexts and functions for the same group of words—dictionary entry and poem, as readers we employ different reading techniques. When we read a dictionary definition, we primarily want to know the meaning of the word. *The American Heritage Dictionary* uses clear organization (designated by the numbered entries) and explanatory examples *("The Peace of Westphalia")* to communicate this information.

But when we read a poem, we read differently. We note the contrast between the title and the first stanza, and we begin to speculate: the word *peace* no longer has meaning and so is obsolete; the world is at the point of death; dictionaries and language no longer have meaning in the modern world. Also, we see in the way the poet has arranged the single-word poetic lines that "hostilities" is contrasted to "freedom."

Because we are reading a poem, we look for different kinds of rhetorical techniques. Our ideas about genre allow us to take the same group of words and read an informative dictionary entry, on the one hand, and an ironic commentary on war, on the other.

Highly specialized genres, such as the sonnet or murder mystery, have more specific rules that the author must follow. A sonnet needs fourteen lines; a murder mystery must have a murder. Once we have identified the context, that is, once we know we are reading a sonnet or a murder mystery, we look for each text's conventional functions. We expect the sonnet to be a highly structured and compressed verbal account of a deep emotion like love; we expect the murder mystery to entertain and intrigue us in its portrayal of an investigator following a pattern of clues to uncover the murderer. Genres help us to read a text by directing our expectations and the interpretive conventions that we employ.

Besides establishing a generic context for our reading, the specific formal qualities of a text also assist us in interpreting its particular meaning. In other words, once we know what formal details to look for in a particular text, we can examine them to see what kinds of meaning they add. In poetry, for example, we might analyze the meter to see how variations emphasize a certain word. Look at the sudden shift in the meter of the third line of Emily Dickinson's poem 49, which I have marked with strong and weak stresses:

U / U / U / U /
I never lost as much but twice,

U / U / U /
And that was in the sod.

/ U U / U / U
Twice have I stood a beggar

U / U / U /
Before the door of God!

The variation of meter at the word "twice" serves to highlight how many times she has already suffered some kind of extreme loss. Not only does the meter break at "twice," but the word's position at the beginning of a line and its appearance at the end of the first line as well add to the emphasis.

In the second stanza of this poem, Dickinson abruptly shifts meter from the soothing iambic pattern (U/) to the more harsh and insistent trochaic pattern (/U):

/ U / U / U
Angels—twice descending

/U / U /
Reimbursed my store—

/ U / U /U
Burglar! Banker—Father!

/U / U /
I am poor once more!

The shift accompanies an increasingly agitated tone suggested by the breakdown of conventional punctuation, the numerous exclamation points, and the accusing cry "Burglar!"

The formal device of the meter helps create both the intellectual content of the poem and its emotional effect. The poetic voice grows increasingly upset by her repeated losses and says through the meter and other formal devices in the second stanza, "I'm angry, God! I've been robbed again!" The details of the form construct the meaning of the text.

Because this poem is highly compressed, its formal features are easy to interpret; but this kind of analysis can be done with all types of literature, as we examine how the author employs or deviates from the conventions of the particular genre in which he or she is working. In a course in literature, you can learn some of these specific ways to read that will help you to understand works of literature more completely.

Formal devices can also function as statements in themselves. When we look at the historical evolution, adaptation, or rejection of certain aspects of genre, we find authors commenting about their values and beliefs through their choice of forms. By following some conventions, by breaking others, and by developing new forms, authors may indicate their vision of life.

In the mid-nineteenth century, the conventional verse form was the iambic pentameter used by the respected earlier poets Shakespeare and Milton. However, Emily Dickinson chose to write her poems primarily in *common meter*, a rhythm and rhyme pattern taken from hymns. Her contemporary Walt Whitman gave up traditional poetry altogether for *free verse*, which has neither meter nor rhyme. The alternative forms that each hewed out in the poetic genre became part of the complex meaning of their poems. Whitman's and Dickinson's rebellion against conventional social and religious ideas included their rebellion against conventional poetic form.

Whitman's philosophy of individual freedom is embodied both in the verse form that he employs and in the content of that verse, which proclaims social, sexual, and emotional freedom. Dickinson's choice of the hymn form may be ironic, in that she uses it to question religious orthodoxy, but her choice may also reflect her creation of a personal religion by replacing the simple, communal sentiments of the hymn with a complex personal statement.

Literary forms are not absolutely connected with certain beliefs; that is, we cannot claim that everyone who uses free verse is a rebel, or that a poet who employs the common meter of hymns must be a Christian. Instead, we must examine the conditions under which an author writes, the social practices that influence the work, and the formal choices that the author has available. The historical context of forms and conventions helps us to understand the philosophical, social, political, and theological implications of literary technique.

Is it Good? Form and Evaluation

The final benefit of formal analysis lies in how it helps us to evaluate literature. Unlike the classical critic, we no longer automatically rank works of literature according to a hierarchy of genres. How should we now sort out good literature from bad? Should we value experimentation or tradition, simplicity or complexity? How can we decide what is good in order to delight in it? Maybe Stephen King is as great an author as Shakespeare and Mohammed Ali's poems are on a par with T. S. Eliot's.

One way to evaluate a particular text is to judge how its specific forms help the text to do what it sets out to do. We have seen how Donald Davie argues that Isaac Watts is a skillful poet because Watts's forms (simple metaphors and diction) fit the function of his poems as hymns. A complex, experimental hymn would be very difficult for the congregation to sing in a meaningful way during a church service. Davie does not say that simplicity is always best, but rather that simplicity best suits this particular kind of verse.

The most useful evaluation acknowledges the criteria on which it is based. It is not very useful to claim, "Shakespeare is a better author than Stephen King." Better at what? If we were to judge the quality of a work by its ability to scare the daylights out of the reader, we might rank King's *It* higher than Shakespeare's *King Lear.* But if we were to judge which work better conveys the agonizing human search for meaning and the complex relationships of parents and children, we most likely would agree that *King Lear* is the better work. On the basis of who uses the simplest, most easily understood vocabulary, King comes out on top. If we look for complex image patterns, allusions, and a more formal vocabulary, Shakespeare is the better author.

Now you may be tempted to argue that it is better to use complex, allusive language and images than a simple style. But that depends on the kind of literary work being produced. A simple style is more appropriate for Isaac Watts's hymns than a complex style, given their purpose as a vehicle for communal worship. A technique appropriate in one context may be totally inappropriate in another. A poet who uses clichés (trite or overused metaphors) in love poems weakens their emotional sincerity and impact. You probably would agree that "Quick as lightning, she became the apple of his eye" is not a particularly moving statement. However, in *The Waste Land,* the poet T. S. Eliot uses clichés effectively to depict the sterility and triteness of modern life.

When we set out to evaluate the aesthetics of a Stephen King novel, then, we need to examine how King uses language and the conventions of the horror story in order to enhance the primary function of a horror story. The fact that Stephen King's *It* does not illuminate the restless human search for meaning does not mean it is not a good horror story. The more important question is whether it achieves the desired emotional effect of absorbing and then scaring the reader. If King's sentence patterns were awkward and stilted, his word choices too predictable, banal, or incongruous, and the "surprise" twist on page 300 already evident by page 30, the reader would lose interest or laugh rather than be engrossed in a crescendo of terror. Stephen King would then have written a bad horror story.

When we read popular fiction, we should still insist on quality of form, but we should recognize that the basis on which we judge aesthetic excellence will differ. We should not apply the same criteria to a horror story or a fantasy as we would to a serious drama, because their primary functions are very different.

These differing functions all have their own value. A Stephen King story unquestionably is much less complex and profound than a Shakespearean drama in terms of what it sets out to do and how it accomplishes that function. *King Lear* delivers much more of an intellectual and emotional challenge, expressing powerful truths and prompting us to think about our life in new ways. Like many of the other great works of literature esteemed by our society, it illuminates some of the major issues of life. However, a Christian can also find value in reading for escape and enjoyment.

Recognizing the genre of a text and its particular formal qualities is thus a key part of the interpretive process. Forms, techniques, and conventions all enhance our interpretation of a text: by signaling what kind of reading skills we should use, by adding intellectual and emotional meanings to the content, by representing historical or philosophical positions in themselves, and by providing one method to evaluate the quality of a text.

One of the major benefits of taking an introductory course in literature is that you become more adept at reading by learning how to analyze and evaluate literature in terms of its formal qualities. What you learn about texts by reading Shakespeare for class during the school year will ultimately inform how you read Stephen King at the beach the next summer.

Archetypal Forms

Although looking at the particular conventions of fiction, poetry, and drama is probably the best known way of discussing the structure of literature, another currently popular approach is to identify common plots, characters, and images that occur repeatedly in all different kinds of literature. These recurring patterns are called *archetypes*. An archetypal approach to literature does not look at the historical evolution of new genres or the changes in convention that different authors make. Instead, such an approach focuses on the similar content of literature from very different times and places.

One common archetype is the pattern of the hero taking a journey. In the *Odyssey*, Odysseus wanders for ten years over unknown oceans, attempting to return home after the Battle of Troy. In the *Divine Comedy*, Dante first descends through nine different circles, or levels, of hell, then ascends through seven levels of Purgatory, and finally travels through the seven circles of medieval astronomy before reaching the Empyrean, or Heaven. A less complicated journey provides the plot structure for *The Adventures of Huckleberry Finn,* in which Huck and the runaway slave Jim float down the Mississippi River in search of freedom.

Other common archetypes include: the god who dies but is reborn, the search for the father, the rags-to-riches Cinderella story, the fatal temptress, the defiant rebel, and purification by water. As you read more, you will discover that these archetypes appear in works as different as Greek myth, Shakespearean drama, Victorian novels, and contemporary poems. Anthropologists have determined that archetypes appear not only in literature but also in ancient religious rituals, folklore, and myth.

A certain group of literary scholars, the *myth critics,* have identified and classified these recurring patterns. The most prominent myth critic, Northrop Frye, argues in his *Anatomy of Criticism* that all literature comes from a "monomyth," a single composite story that follows the seasonal cycle of spring, summer, fall, and winter. All literature, according to Frye, falls into four genres—comedy, romance, tragedy, and satire—which reflect the archetypal myths associated with the four seasons. Comedy (the story of spring) follows the hero from rags to riches. Tragedy (the story of fall) tells of the fall from happiness to catastrophe. Romance (the story of summer) pictures an ideal dream world, and satire (the story of winter) shows an imperfect world of captivity and frustration.

Where Do They Come From?

Many people believe that archetypes represent some kind of elemental, universal pattern deep within all human beings. The psychologist Carl G. Jung argues that the human race has a "collective unconscious" that contains the "psychic residue" of experiences in the lives of our ancient ancestors. Archetypes appear in myths, religions, dreams, and literature because they are unconsciously carried deep within everyone's psyche.

Northrop Frye suggests that archetypes arise from the universal human desire for identity and order, which is fulfilled in romance and comedy but stymied or depicted ironically in tragedy and satire. Frye thinks literature forms a communal dream world:

In ordinary life we fall into a private and separate subconscious every night, where we reshape the world according to a private and separate imagination. Underneath literature there's another kind of subconscious, which is social and not private, a need for forming a community around certain symbols, like the Queen and the flag, or around certain gods that represent order and stability, or becoming and change, or death and rebirth to a new life. (*Educated*, 103)

Jung and Frye agree that authors have no choice but to write using archetypes. Unconsciously, all authors will tap into the archetypal world, so literary works are not so much the production of the particular author as involuntary expressions. Frye claims, "It takes a great deal of will power to write poetry, but part of that will power must be employed in trying to relax the will, so making a large part of one's writing involuntary" (*Anatomy*, 88). He continues, "The true father or shaping spirit of the poem is the form of the poem itself, and this form is a manifestation of the universal spirit of poetry" (*Anatomy*, 98). Jung and Frye both believe that archetypes completely control the forms that all literature takes.

C. S. Lewis adopts a different approach. Although he does not believe that all literature is based on archetypes, Lewis identifies commonly recurring plots and characters stemming from ancient myth and often employs such formulas in his own work. In *Till We Have Faces*, Lewis retells the classical myth of Cupid and Psyche, while much in *The Chronicles of Narnia* comes from British folklore about elves, witches, druids, and dragons.

Lewis believes that these kinds of myths are powerful because mythic patterns are based on God's absolute truth. When a story contains an archetype, its author is not drawing on the universal unconscious or the monomyth, but rather on God's truth, whether she or he is aware of it or not. A voice in *The Pilgrim's Regress* asks,

"Was there any age in any land when men did not know that corn and wine were the blood and body of a dying and yet living God?" (171). Lewis would say that the image of corn and wine and the motif of the dying yet living God are universally significant because of their origin in Christian reality.

For Lewis, the Bible provides the original archetypes, even for those myths that predate its history, which foreshadow the Christian reality. All dying god motifs—from the Fisher King of ancient fertility rituals to the slaughter of Aslan in Lewis's own *The Lion, the Witch, and the Wardrobe*—come from and reflect Christ's death. In contrast, Jung and Frye believe that the story of Christ is only one of a number of similar stories that all reflect the same archetype.

The Usefulness of Archetypes

Archetypes of some kind or other do exist in a great deal of literature. Their major value seems to lie in how they evoke common human experience and so provide a way for us to understand a work from a different culture and time. Archetypes show us how much we have in common with other people, and so give us the means by which we can see ourselves in works of literature.

The Bible has many recurring patterns. The image of bread as a sustainer of life appears in the celebration of passover, the miracle of manna in the wilderness, the feeding of the five thousand, and the institution of communion. Such archetypal patterns are always connected to historical events. When Jesus claims, "I am the bread of life," he reminds his followers of other occasions on which God had provided salvation for his people. The image of bread as salvation originates in the world of time and space.

However, as we think about the universality of the bread image, we might consider the fact that some Bible translators believe that a more meaningful translation for native South American readers is, "I am the banana of life." In some cultures, bread has no meaning. Lewis's example from *The Pilgrim's Regress* depicts the primary sustainer of life as corn (which is also used to make bread). Perhaps corn or bread are universal images of physical sustenance not so much because Christ instituted the Lord's Supper using bread but because of the physical nature of the world that God created. We need food to survive, and for many of us, bread is a staple of our diet. Christ instituted the Lord's Supper using bread because it was a readily understandable image.

Perhaps archetypes originate out of common human experience and so reflect God's structuring hand in history. They are not so much part of our ancestral memory or a communal dream world as they are ways that all human beings respond to God's world. We all get hungry; we all feel the need for salvation; we all are tempted. As human beings continually repeat these experiences, they discover helpful metaphors and narratives with which to represent them. For different cultures, the particular images may differ, ranging from bread to bananas.

While we can acknowledge that literature does have many recurring patterns, we must also carefully examine the implications of archetypal theories. Frye's approach to archetypes is very deterministic. His belief that the author is primarily an unconscious transmitter does not allow for as much self-expression or intentional action on the part of the author as we might wish. His theory encroaches on the Christian concept of the person as a unique individual.

Secondly, Frye tends to overlook or downplay the relationship between the real (historical) world and the world of archetypes. He claims, "we relate the poems and plays and novels we read and see, not to the men who wrote them, nor even directly to ourselves; we relate them to each other" (Anatomy, 73). In this special world of literature, "things are removed just out of reach of belief and action" (Anatomy, 78). Such an approach to archetypes can make literature trivial and irrelevant to life.

Observing the archetypes in literature has limited benefits. It is interesting to find these common patterns, but once we have identified them, what do we do with them? Do they add meaning to the text or somehow enhance the reading experience? Identifying the archetypes sometimes only strips away the individuality of a text and exposes its resemblance to every other text. Myth critics argue that archetypes are effective because they move us at a primitive or subconscious level. This may be true, but a primitive response to literature does not necessarily help us to serve God or love our neighbors.

We do not necessarily find archetypes in every work of literature. The theory works much better with narrative than it does with lyric or expository prose. Similarly, fantasy and fairy tales seem to carry far more archetypal references than realistic fiction.

A Christian considering archetypes must think about them as somehow falling within God's creation and ordering of the world. Whether we think archetypes originate in the particulars of the Christian story, as C. S. Lewis proposes, or in the way that God has given human beings certain common experiences, we must acknowledge that God's rule extends to archetypes. Similarly, we must think about archetypes in a way that recognizes the individuality of the author and sees literature as a means of communication. Finally, as responsible readers, we must see our activity of reading as a way for us to act in the world. An archetypal approach that relegates literature to an imaginative dream world is unacceptable.

Chapter 13

GENRES AND THE CHRISTIAN FAITH: METAFICTION, COMEDY, AND TRAGEDY

As we attempt to choose wisely what we read, one of our decisions will involve the genres of literature. Given a choice of several kinds of literature, most of us would probably prefer to read fiction. After all, narrative is a central part of our faith and our life. Our Christian beliefs are based on the narrative of God's dealings with Israel and on the story of Jesus's life, death, and resurrection. We hear bedtime stories as children, learn biblical stories in Sunday school, and watch narratives unfold on our television and movie screens. Because stories are so familiar to us, many of us would choose to read a novel before tackling a book of essays or poetry. Although it is understandable, our preference for fiction should not keep us from sampling some of the many other kinds of literature. Reading choices might be like eating choices: if you stick with the familiar, you miss discovering new delights.

However, when we consider that certain forms of literature have philosophical implications, we may wonder about the relationships that different genres have to our Christian faith. In deciding what we read, should we take into account the philosophical perspective suggested by the genre? The question of the congruence of particular genres with the Christian faith is also an important issue for the aspiring writer who is a Christian. Are some genres more appropriate for a Christian to use than others?

The historical development of genres represents one of the ways that human beings have worked out the literary potentials of God's creation. Genres' constant evolution is not necessarily either good or bad: we should neither expect the development of a Perfect Genre during our lifetime nor long nostalgically for the good old days when genres were not corrupted. As writers have developed the possibilities of language and structure, they have made some good choices and some bad ones.

The example of the Bible shows that God appreciates the variety of genres developed by human beings out of the material given them by the Creator's original activity. God did not inspire his writers to create completely new genres of literature, but instead had them work within established genres such as wisdom literature, Hebrew poetry, parables, historical narratives, and apocalyptic literature.

As biblical authors wrote in the genres common to their culture, they adapted the genres to their own purpose (which was God's inspired purpose). For example, biblical scholars point to the gospel as a new form that was apparently developed out of other kinds of writing for the particular purpose of depicting the life and work of Christ. God's employment of existing genres in the Bible suggests that some of the particular ways humans have developed God's creation can help assist his purposes in the world.

The philosophical intentions and implications underlying different genres undoubtedly result in some that are more compatible with Christian understanding than others. Genres may specifically affirm, generally agree with, or blatantly oppose Christian concepts. However, these differences do not mean that we should read only those works that affirm our perspective. To encounter ideas with which we disagree either in part or in total can be a valuable experience.

To get a better idea of how genres and the Christian faith affect each other, let's examine three specific genres and evaluate them with reference to our Christian understanding. First, we will consider an extreme development of modern narrative form called metafiction in order to press the question of how Christians can find value in a genre with which they philosophically disagree. Then, we will look at the common genres of comedy and tragedy in order to determine how congruent each is with a Christian vision of life and how helpful each is to the Christian reader.

Metafiction and the Christian

Metafiction is a relatively new kind of narrative form that can appear in a short story, novel, or drama. It is fiction about the nature of fiction. John Barth's "Life-Story," for example, is about an author writing a story about an author writing a story about, and so forth. Metafictional stories often violate our normal expectations that fiction will have a coherent plot, identifiable characters, and a clear narrative perspective.

Other popular metafictional writers include Samuel Beckett, Donald Barthelme, Kurt Vonnegut, Jr., and Jorge Luis Borges. Most literature anthologies today include at least one story or play that might be termed metafiction, although because it is a recent generic development that is still being defined, an editor might describe this genre as "postmodern fiction" or "absurdist fiction."

Crazy, unexpected, frustrating, intriguing—all are ways one might describe metafiction. Some readers enjoy the bizarre humor and twists that such literature provides, much like the parodies and spoofs on *Saturday Night Live*. Others wonder why they should bother reading this confusing stuff. One reason is that metafiction is an extremely important generic development in terms of the philosophical view it represents. Metafiction represents a literary response to and comment on a modern philosophical development called *epistemological skepticism.*

What people believe they can know about the world (their epistemology, literally, "the science of knowing") directly influences the kind of stories they write. For example, in the eighteenth century (often called the age of reason), the realistic novel was the latest innovation. People then believed that a coherent universe existed that could be known through the experience of sense data. Consequently, they wrote literature that imitated reality as they saw it, with detailed descriptions, true-to-life characters, and orderly plots based on cause and effect. The realistic novel expressed in its form the ordered reality of the eighteenth-century world.

Let's turn now to the twentieth century and to the new skeptical epistemology, which simply means increasing uncertainty about what we can know. Many scientific and psychological studies have contributed to this uncertainty. With the decline of belief in absolute truth, the notion arises that humans are fiction makers who develop systems (fictions) through which they see and order their knowledge of the universe. These systems are all shaped by language. Instead of perceiving reality and then using language to describe it, humans actually call reality into being and order their perceptions into some coherent state by using language. Meaning is created by language, according to this philosophy.

Metafiction emerges out of these philosophical developments as contemporary authors insist that the old fictional technique of *mimesis,* that is, the imitation of reality, can no longer be valid in an age in which we are no longer sure what reality is and must create it ourselves. Metafiction exposes the fictionality of reality by telling a story about another story (in a parody), a story about characters creating a fiction, or a story about how meaning systems are generated.

For example, in Robert Coover's *The Universal Baseball Association, Inc.,* the character Henry Waugh creates a game of baseball with a cast of characters ruled by his throw of the dice. He develops personalities for his players and stories of their off-field behavior. After establishing this context, the narrative moves from Waugh to focus on the events within the world he creates.

Metafictions invariably show that fictions will break down: some fictions may be useful for a time, but ultimately they prove inadequate. Waugh's fiction goes out of control when the dice shows that his favorite baseball player is to be killed by a bean ball. If all fictions will break down, so will metafiction. Consequently, these stories are full of deliberate artificiality and irony. The author may stop to comment on the story, to give the reader alternative possibilities for

action, or to joke, pun and parody. This uninhibited self-reflective-
ness adds an element of play and uncertainty.

The skeptical epistemology and consequent playfulness of metafiction also gives rise to a new view of what literature is and how it
works. Literature no longer imitates reality; it is an addition to reality
in the form of a linguistic object. The critic William H. Gass advises:
"The novelist . . . will keep us kindly imprisoned in his language—
there is literally nothing beyond" (*Fiction*, 8).

In Gass's view a novel is a fictional system of signs with no necessary relationship to the world. Instead of telling you something, it
makes you experience something. Instead of creating order, it offers
itself to be ordered. Another metafiction writer, Raymond Federman,
explains:

The reader will be the one who extracts, invents, creates a meaning and an
order. . . . And it is this total participation in the creation which will give
the reader a sense of having created meaning and not having simply received,
passively, a neatly prearranged meaning. (14)

Fiction about fiction-making forces us into fiction-making ourselves.

Given these philosophical premises, how should a Christian respond? As believers in absolute truth, in the authoritative and con-
trolling hand of God, should we be reading works written in a genre
that denies those basic beliefs? Is metafiction immoral?

Christians need to be familiar with the major intellectual movements in the world so that they can carry on an intelligent dialogue
with others. For this reason alone, Christians should read and study
metafiction, for it is an important twentieth-century development.
However, metafiction can also teach us much about our world and
ourselves. This genre can help us to understand meaning systems:
how they are created, how they become inadequate, and how they
can be used up. Scrutinizing meaning systems more closely will help
us to distinguish the good from the bad in the systems we develop
as we seek to live in God's world in a manner pleasing to him.

Another valuable contribution that metafiction makes is its expo-
sure of decayed and cliché-ridden language. As language has evolved,

humans have often made poor choices and warped and distorted the linguistic gifts of the Lord. We may easily see how obscene, profane, and cruel language warps God's gift; but jargon, slogans, trite expressions, and mindless phrases equally degrade a rich potential. Metafiction exposes such language humorously and playfully, and this sense of joy and playfulness that it evokes is valuable, especially when it teaches us to laugh at ourselves and our errors.

One of the major differences between metafiction and realistic fiction is that the former makes us experience something for ourselves, while the latter tells us about that same experience by depicting it in the life of a character. So, rather than simply show us an upset, bereaved son who can't find meaning in his life, Donald Barthelme's metafictional mystery, "Views of my Father Weeping," upsets us, yanks meaning out of our hands, and murders our expectation of a resolution to the mystery thus giving us an experience of confusion and bereavement. But is it wrong to make us experience rather than to tell us? Experience is a form of knowledge; tacit learning is every bit as valuable as explicit learning.

Even though metafictional writers want to claim that their texts are independent linguistic objects with no relation to the real world, we can see that such texts represent their authors' strategy for participating in the world. In a rather round-about way, metafictionalists imitate reality as they perceive it; their reality is a complex web of fiction-making and fiction-collapsing, a constant process of a person's imposing meaning on his or her world. As these writers make and destroy fictions and draw their readers into the fictional process, they demonstrate one way in which we can wield textual power and participate in our world.

Probably we will disagree most significantly with metafiction's denial of absolute truth. Although we may acknowledge the uncertainty of meaning systems, we have a hope of someday finding an absolute. We never doubt the existence of a Reality; we only doubt our ability to know that Reality completely in a world of sin and error.

When we probe the philosophical bases and the practical functions of the new genre of metafiction, we find much that it can teach us.

Even though we clearly disagree with metafictionalists on key points, we may also appropriate new ways of thinking from them.

This discussion of the relatively new genre of metafiction suggests some of the ways that Christians can and should interact with a genre of literature. Even genres that represent extreme philosophical positions with which we strongly disagree can provide us with valuable ways to participate in the world responsibly.

Comedy, Tragedy, and the Christian Vision

Suppose you go to the theater one evening without knowing anything about the play you are going to see. Arriving late and dashing madly for your seat before the lights dim, you neglect to pick up a program. Just as you find your place next to the friend you were meeting, the theater darkens and the curtain goes up. "What's this play about?" you murmur to your companion, who shrugs, annoyed at your lateness. In complete ignorance, you turn your attention to the stage. How will you ever tell if you are watching a comedy or a tragedy?

This is probably not a question that would bother many of us, simply because we all can tell the difference instinctively. Comedy makes us laugh; tragedy makes us cry. But what causes these two very different effects? The English poet Lord Byron provides an answer in *Don Juan:* "All tragedies are finished by a death, / All comedies are ended by a marriage." But even before you reach the end, you probably can tell if you are watching a comedy or a tragedy. A certain kind of conclusion, plot pattern or hero does not insure that a play is a comedy or a tragedy. The two kinds of drama differ less in their form or structure than in their perspective on the story they tell.

The comic and tragic are two of the most familiar and enduring perspectives in literature. Originally, comedy and tragedy were strictly defined forms of Greek drama, but over the centuries, these forms developed and expanded in many ways. Comic and tragic perspectives now appear in many literary forms other than the drama. Often we tend to think that tragedy is superior to comedy, but the historical development of literature shows that comedy and tragedy evolved together and often appear as complementary units. Both provide worthwhile insights for the Christian reader.

Classical Tragedy and Romantic Comedy

In his *Poetics*, Aristotle gives the exact specifications for a tragedy: it is a serious drama portraying a hero of a highly moral but flawed character, who aspires to greatness but encounters suffering and defeat. Although the tragedy ends disastrously for the hero, some kind of cosmic reconciliation allows the audience to experience *catharsis*, or purgation, of the emotions of pity and terror that they have experienced.

Aristotle's discussion of comedy unfortunately has not survived, but the common pattern of early comedy in ancient literature features a realistic hero who encounters an obstacle (often in his or her love life), overcomes it, and lives happily ever after. The comedy ends with a celebration that brings most of the characters into a happy social circle. We are amused and entertained by such plots. These two structural patterns make up what we often call *classical tragedy* and *romantic comedy*.

Over the course of time, authors have modified or completely changed the forms of classical tragedy and romantic comedy. Some variations serve to narrow formal elements: the Elizabethan revenge tragedy, for example, follows the classical pattern but also requires that the hero pursue a quest for vengeance and that the action include murder, mutilation, and bloody mayhem. (The popular film series *Nightmare on Elm Street* is a kind of modern revenge tragedy.) Other variations expand or change the formal characteristics: modern tragedy may feature a common, middle-class protagonist, like the salesman Willy Loman in Arthur Miller's *Death of a Salesman*, and it often omits the cosmic reconciliation typical of classical tragedy. The subject matter of modern comedy has expanded greatly from that of romantic comedy and now includes stories such as characters watching a play they are in (Tom Stoppard's *Rosencrantz and Guildenstern are Dead*), soldiers experiencing the insanity of World War

II (Joseph Heller's *Catch-22*), or the interactions of modern families *(The Cosby Show).*

Up until this point we have been considering comedy and tragedy primarily as dramatic forms, but as the genres evolved, they often took on completely new forms. A tragedy no longer has to be a play: we find tragic poems (Robert Frost's "The Death of the Hired Hand"), short stories (Stephen Crane's "The Open Boat"), and novels (F. Scott Fitzgerald's *The Great Gatsby*). The movement from tragedy (a noun) to tragic (an adjective) indicates what the critic Alastair Fowler calls a shift from a *kind* (or genre) of literature to a *mode* of literature. As *kinds* of literature change over time, they often expand into *modes,* no longer restricted to an exact formal pattern but still evoking the mood and vision of the earlier *kind.*

The comic and tragic modes or perspectives embody two very different views of life. As Christians we may wonder how we should react to these two modes. Should a Christian laugh or cry? When we analyze the different visions of life embodied in each mode, we can see how comedy and tragedy represent dialogical halves (two parts in dialogue) of the all-encompassing Christian view of life.

Comic and Tragic Visions

In order to understand the difference between the comic and the tragic vision, let's return to classical tragedy and romantic comedy. The same general plot or kind of character can be either comic or tragic, depending on the perspective from which it is viewed. Shakespeare uses the plot of an old foolish man whose pride causes his downfall in both *King Lear* and *The Merry Wives of Windsor.* But the different perspectives from which he views Lear and Falstaff and their different physical fates result in one play being called tragedy and the other comedy. The comic and tragic differ in their perspectives on human failure and its consequences in our earthly existence.

Take the familiar routine of a woman slipping on a banana peel. In a comedy, a woman slips on a banana peel right in front of a very attractive man. Humiliated, she believes all chances for a romance are destroyed. However, through a series of coincidences, the two meet again, fall in love, and eventually marry. In the comic perspective, the woman's clumsiness contrasts our common desire for dignity with the equally common way our bodies fail us. We laugh, but we know the woman will not be permanently affected by her fall; the comic vision does not acknowledge lasting pain or sorrow.

But if she slips, hits her head and dies, and the town council bans littering in an ordinance named after her, the story becomes tragic. The failure has serious consequences, and the final social order does not include her physically: she may live on either eternally or in fame but not on this earth.

The comic vision looks at human action as a spectacle of limitations. Some of those limitations arise from our undeniable physical natures. We have bodies that embarrass us: we slip on banana peels; we burp when meeting our new in-laws; we mix up our words when we are excited. In Shakespeare's *A Midsummer Night's Dream,* a group of workmen perform a play, and in their nervousness come out with such lines as, "I see a voice! Now will I to the chink,/To spy an I can hear my Thisby's face" (V.i.190–91).

Other limitations come from our character flaws. We are vain and strive for ridiculous things: In *The Cosby Show,* Theo Huxtable paints a mustache on his upper lip in order to impress girls, while his sister Vanessa secretly applies makeup in defiance of her parents' ban. The romantic comedy looks specifically at the foolish things we do in pursuit of love, but all comedies highlight some kind of human foolishness.

Still other limitations are imposed on us by our world. Our best laid plans go wrong. Banana peels strew our paths. In Shakespeare's comedies, parents forbid marriages, storms and shipwreck drive lovers apart, or a magic potion makes a fairy queen love an ass. Modern romantic comedies similarly depict obstacles to love: the Gatekeeper in search of the Keymaster inconveniently possesses the object of Bill Murray's pursuit in *Ghostbusters,* while an inopportune phone call heralding a new clue often keeps David and Maddie apart in *Moonlighting.*

By exposing our many limitations, the comic vision makes us laugh—but also think—about our vices and excesses, our finite human condition. When it makes an individual or institution look ridiculous in order to criticize or condemn it, comedy becomes *satiric*. The element of satire in comedy varies, but depending on its degree, the comic vision can correct human folly and vice by providing important insights into life along with its humor.

In *The Adventures of Huckleberry Finn*, Huck lives briefly with a family waging a traditional Southern feud, who take time out from shooting their neighbors to attend church. Huck tells us, "It was pretty ornery preaching—all about brotherly love, and such-like tiresomeness; but everybody said it was a good sermon, and they all talked it over going home." Mark Twain makes these people look ridiculous through their church-going in order to criticize their hypocrisy and the senselessness of a feud based on a false notion of "honor."

After exposing human limitations, the comic vision depicts endurance, love, and reconciliation. Comedies end happily and affirm community: lovers are united, families enjoy meals together, ghostbusters emerge from their final battle to receive the cheers of the multitude. In *The Merry Wives of Windsor*, Falstaff looks extremely foolish when he cavorts through Windsor Forest disguised as a buck to meet the women he fancies are in love with him. But after his folly is exposed, he is invited to the final community dinner to "laugh this sport o'er by a country fire" (V.v. 229). The final order in the comic vision is celebratory and includes the hero.

The comic vision affirms material existence. In its perspective on human failure, comedy reminds us, as the critic Nathan A. Scott, Jr., says, "of how deeply rooted we are in all the tangible things of this world" (28). The comic vision points to but also celebrates our physical nature, our personality flaws, our susceptibility to chance. It suggests that through love and reconciliation, we will endure. Suzanne Langer notes that the comic vision celebrates life: "it is an image of human vitality holding its own in the world amid the surprises of unplanned coincidence" (331). The emphasis on social order and celebration suggests that human endurance is a community effort, that vitality is best preserved in social bonds.

The sheer enthusiasm embodied in the comic means that we laugh at things that we would never laugh at in real life. In Francois Truffaut's film *Shoot the Piano Player* (1960), a gangster attempts to impress a boy with stories of the many crimes he has committed. The boy protests, "You're making all this up!" The gangster swears, "May my mother die if I am lying." Sure enough, the next scene shows an old woman toppling backward in her chair, before the camera cuts back to the gangster. This scene is funny, not because death is funny, but because its focus is on the braggadocio of the gangster rather than on the agony of the woman's death.

The tragic vision, on the other hand, directs our attention toward the suffering caused by human failure. Like the comic vision, it points out our human limitations, but these limitations stem more from moral flaws than from our physical nature. King Lear's foolishness causes him to make a serious error with respect to governing his kingdom, and his pride encourages him to think he can still be treated like a king without the authority of the position behind him. These are moral flaws. Falstaff, in comparison, is foolish in his relationships with women, and his pride lies in his imagined sexual prowess. His moral flaws manifest themselves in his obese, aged, yet lecherous body.

The tragic vision also has a different perspective on circumstances. Chance will temporarily interfere and block the hero's intentions in comedy, but in tragedy, circumstances work continually to keep heroes from attaining their goals. We enjoy, laugh at, and eventually overcome the limits of the human condition in comedy; but in tragedy, these limits represent insurmountable obstacles.

The tragic provides a very different view of human beings from the comic. Humans have dignity, even in their defeat. Our errors doom us, circumstances work against us, but we continue to struggle and to aspire to our goals. This does not mean that the hero will always be of high stature, as in classical tragedy. Everyday folk demonstrate admirable courage and persistence in the vicissitudes of life: Willy

Loman desperately tries to keep his family together and to achieve the success of the American dream in *Death of a Salesman;* Amanda wants only the best for her crippled daughter Laura in *The Glass Menagerie.* The hero need not always be the most admirable character either: Macbeth has few redeeming qualities to counter his bloody ambition, but he displays courage and dignity in his warped drive to be king.

In place of the love and reconciliation found in the comic, the tragic results in hurt and alienation. The misguided hopes, the moral failures, the errors in judgment, the constraints of circumstance—all result in suffering and defeat. When Willy Loman realizes his responsibility for his son's aimlessness and despair, he commits suicide in order to leave his family his insurance money. Hamlet's desire for revenge separates him from his mother, his lover Ophelia, and his school friends. The tragic vision tells stories that conclude with death, madness, imprisonment, maiming, or endless sorrow. Unlike the comic, the human limitations depicted in the tragic have irreversible physical consequences.

The final social order in the tragic vision excludes the hero. Falstaff may be invited to the merry wives' dinner and fire, but Lear dies before the kingdom reaches peace under a new ruler. In tragedy, the final order comes from the gods or society putting the pieces back together after the hero's defeat. The hero may have achieved a moral and eternal victory, but he or she has been defeated temporally. Thus, the emphasis in the tragic is not so much on social reconciliation as it is on individual persistence and eternal reconciliation.

Probably one of the major differences between classical tragedy and much modern tragedy is the omission of the final imposition of order. Modern tragedy seldom provides someone to take control and put society back together after the disruptions of the tragic. Cosmic reconciliation is missing from the modern tragic vision, which, because it no longer recognizes any cosmic or moral power that might impose order and achieve peace, ends in despair or a personal leap of faith. But even when order is reimposed, as in classical tragedy, the protagonist does not take part in it. He or she may grow morally as a result of suffering but will not participate in the final social reconciliation.

The Dialogics of Comic and Tragic

Given the fact that the comic and the tragic embody such different perspectives, we often compare their relative worth and end up exalting the tragic viewpoint. Agonizing over moral dilemmas somehow seems more worthwhile than laughing at the foibles of humanity or enjoying a fairy-tale ending. Numerous literary critics argue that tragedy is the greater genre, more significant than lightweight comedy. Surely an evening pondering the profound tragedy of *Hamlet* is better spent than an evening laughing at the romantic confusions and verbal duels of Beatrice and Benedick in Shakespeare's *Much Ado About Nothing*. Or is it?

Christians have often debated the relative values of the comic and tragic, and we can find advocates for both sides. Because of the common assumption that tragedy is more profound and raises more important moral questions, several authors have discussed the compatibility of Christianity and tragedy. Probably the greatest proponent of the congruence of Christianity and tragedy is the Shakespearean critic G. Wilson Knight, who argues that the structure of classical tragedy follows the basic Christian story with the hero representing a type of Christ who suffers, dies, and has a kind of resurrection in the final cosmic reconciliation.

Leland Ryken takes another kind of approach when he argues that the biblical story of the fall is the source and model for all subsequent tragedy (96). Like Knight, he concentrates on classical tragedy, defining tragedy as following a particular pattern of action in which an admirable hero makes the wrong choice, suffers, and dies. Ryken believes that the tragic hero often attains a moral victory in his final recognition of his error or sin. For the most part, though, literary critics have seen the tragic vision as incompatible with the Christian assurance of a happy ending.

More readers have affirmed the comic vision to be congruent with Christianity. Nelvin Vos argues that the movement from estrangement to reconciliation in the structure of comedy parallels that of the entire biblical narrative: "What uniquely marks both the religious and the comic worlds is the experience of reconciliation, the movement from loss and alienation to the arrival of 'at-one-ment' with self, society, nature, and the infinite" (113). The comic story, according to Vos, represents the Christian understanding of existence as embodied in the doctrine of salvation.

Nathan A. Scott, Jr., on the other hand, sees the comic as affirming the doctrines of the Creation and Incarnation, in which God indicated the worth of the material world. In its celebration of the concrete things of this world, comedy reminds us of the value of our creaturely existence:

[The comedian] will not let us forget that we are men, that we are finite and conditioned creatures—not angels. And, in its deeply affirmative attitude toward the created orders of existence, in the profound 'materialism' of its outlook, the comic imagination . . . summarizes an important part of the Christian testimony about the meaning of human life. (38)

In considering the relative merits of the tragic and the comic, we must first remember that solemnity is not intrinsically better than laughter. God creates us with the capacity for both sorrow and joy, and he calls us both to weep with those who mourn and to celebrate with those who delight in his gifts. Second, we need to acknowledge that the comic vision has a deeper perspective that underlies its entertainment. Something can be both funny and serious. Often the comic exposes human folly in such a way as to advocate more responsible human action. We laugh, but we also learn not to be greedy, or vain, or hypocritical. Comedy can provide both personal and social correction through its satiric vision.

When we hold the tragic and comic perspectives up against the Christian view, we find that they form two opposing but complementary halves that, combined, suggest our own more comprehensive perspective. As such, they are in constant dialogue with each other, challenging and reaffirming each other.

The way that tragedy and comedy originally appeared together suggests their complementary nature. In the tradition of classical Greek drama, a tragic trilogy was always followed by a satyr play, which developed the motifs of the tragedies from a comic perspective. In his extensive survey of ancient literature and art, the Russian critic M. M. Bakhtin points to "the attempt to accompany every tragic (or serious) treatment of material with a parallel comic (parodic-travestying) treatment" (56). For example, in two frescoes facing each other in Pompeii, one shows a heroic Perseus rescuing the lovely maiden Andromeda, while the other tells the same story from a comic perspective by portraying peasants armed with sticks and stones attempting to help a naked bathing woman with a snake wrapped around her (57).

In later dramatic forms, the mutual dependence of comedy and tragedy occurs within a single kind of literature. Instead of tragic trilogy and satyr play, we now find the hybrid tragicomedy and the infusion of tragic perspectives into comedies and comic perspective into tragedies. In Shakespeare's *The Comedy of Errors*, Egeon receives a death sentence at the outset that is removed only at the end of the play; in *Much Ado About Nothing*, Hero apparently dies of shame when her lover falsely accuses her of unfaithfulness at their marriage altar. Similarly, tragedies may have brief moments of comic levity, as when the gravediggers in *Hamlet* toss skulls about while philosophizing about human mortality.

The comic and the tragic thus form what Bakhtin calls a "dialogical system," in which two different perspectives animate each other. The comic and the tragic are two halves of a conversation, a dialogue as it were, in which one part gives rise to and highlights the other part. For Bakhtin, the function of the comic, in particular, is to suggest that reality is fuller, richer, and more contradictory than the tragic allows. The tragic vision establishes a narrowly defined view of the world focusing on errors, suffering, loss, and death; without denying the reality of that vision, the comic perspective allows us to see the rich variety of other conditions and experiences of life. It is as though the tragic vision claims, "here's the way that humans experience life: our efforts on this earth end in catastrophe"; and the comic responds, "Yes. But at other times things work out. We achieve reconcilation, love, and community. Our efforts are comically ineffective but do not seriously harm us." Reality offers more options, possibilities, and perspectives than those of tragedy.

Christians understand that richer and more contradictory view. Christianity is a religion full of such tensions: this world is not our final home, but we are to cultivate it responsibly; we are full of sin, but we are the crown jewels of God's creation; we are incapable of responding to God through our own strength, but God calls us to accept his free gift of salvation. We recognize the numerous paradoxes that inform our life on this earth, and we affirm human existence even while knowing that without God's help it is doomed.

The differing perspectives of the comic and the tragic represent two ways to look at life that we hold in constant tension with each other. The comic emphasis on the physical and on human limitation affirms our material and historical nature, but the tragic attention to these limitations acknowledges the pain that they can produce. Our understanding of the end of the plot depends on whether we are standing close in temporal time or stepping back to examine eternity. In the comic, human problems are resolved in historical time: we are invited to the feast; we marry the hero; we bear many daughters and sons. The comic suggests that earthly tragedy is not inevitable, that often things do work out in this world, and we attain important moments of joy in situations of love and community. But the disastrous temporal conclusion to tragedy shows that life on this earth can also be tragic. Many people, including Christians, will suffer and die, even if they achieve an eternal reconciliation.

Christians recognize the truth that each perspective carries. The Bible tells stories of earthly happiness as well as earthly failure: Ruth marries Boaz and gives birth to the grandfather of David, but Stephen is dragged out of the city and stoned to death by an angry mob.

When we look at life from the perspective of human time, we cannot guarantee either a happy or sad resolution.

However, when we take an eternal perspective, we can see that our errors and suffering will eventually result in reconciliation and victory. Christ will return to end human time and establish his eternal kingdom. Although we may lose all of our possessions, our dignity, and our life on this earth, yet if we believe in God and his promises, we will achieve eternal life.

When we look at the earthly reconciliation inevitable in the comic from the eternal perspective, we see it as analogous to our belief in ultimate reconciliation. Things *will* work out; we will live happily ever after. The cosmic reconciliation of classical tragedy also affirms the eternal perspective of Christianity, but the modern version of tragedy that ends in despair denies the existence of the eternal. We may attempt to understand and sympathize with those who view life in this way, but such a vision is obviously incompatible with a Christian understanding.

The final dynamically opposed aspect of the comic and the tragic lies in the focus of the one on social existence and of the other on individual responsibility. The comic affirms the value of the social unit as composed in marriage, family, or kingdom. Our human limitations at times interfere in the successful establishment of these life-sustaining institutions, but eventually the forces of life triumph and society reforms and endures. The tragic, on the other hand, concentrates on the struggle of the individual to succeed in a world riddled with difficulty. It celebrates the persistence and aspiration of the individual despite alienation and loneliness.

In a similar manner, Christians acknowledge the importance of both the individual and the group, the Christian person and the Christian community. Our moral choices are first personal—whether we believe in Jesus Christ as our Savior—but then quickly become communal as we struggle to live peacefully and justly with the others who share God's world with us. Our own moral responsibilities are both individual and communal; therefore, both the comic and the tragic emphasis are valuable for us.

A dialogical approach to the comic and tragic, then, recognizes the different emphasis of each mode as well as the longstanding interconnection of the two. The tragic and the comic represent two ways of viewing the consequences of human effort and the nature of human existence that are in constant tension with each other. The rich reality of life as Christians understand it means that, paradoxically, our existence on this earth is both a success and a failure. We will end our days both with the death of our body and with the marriage feast of the Lamb.

CONCLUSION

Throughout this book, the two of us have examined literature as a form of human action. The writing and reading of literary works are important ways that men and women can act as responsible agents in God's world. By viewing literature as a form of human action, we acknowledge that there are many uses that can be made of language in general, and of the language of literature in particular. A poem may express the feelings of its author and seek to give pleasure to its reader, but it may also do any number of other things: record the history of a people, impart information about the natural world, or inspire its audience to take proper action on a crucial issue.

In seeing literature as a form of human action, this book has disagreed with certain modern beliefs about literature and has pressed a case for seeing it as a product of history as well as a participant in history. Whenever a person attempts to define literature, for example, he or she makes use of a number of implicit beliefs about the nature of reality and the nature of language. In turn, these beliefs represent historical developments in established traditions of thought. The Christian student of literature ought to recognize that many modern assumptions about literature grew out of intellectual traditions that challenged the central beliefs of orthodox Christianity.

A Christian understanding of literature ought to be grounded in doctrines derived from the Scriptures and developed through the course of Christian history. One goal of this book has been to show the centrality of key doctrines in a Christian view of literature. For example, the doctrines of Creation and Redemption informed the description of literature given near the end of the first chapter: "a vital means we have of responding to the order, beauty, and grace of God and his world and to the disorder that our sin has brought into that world."

Throughout this book, the view of literature as a form of human action in history has been coupled with the belief that the differences between literature and other forms of action are differences of degree rather than kind. We saw how metaphor and story are not the exclusive property of poets and fiction writers but are present in all uses of language. Furthermore, we explored ways in which literary genres and modes such as tragedy and comedy help not only to organize the history of literature but to reveal vital truths about human experience in God's world.

In addition to looking at the history of modern views of literature and examining the nature of its language and forms, we have considered what happens in the experience of reading. To that end, we have explored questions about what actually takes place when we sit down to read a book and we have thought through some of the implications of the conflict of interpretations. We have also paid considerable attention to the ways we can evaluate the form of a literary work as well as the ethical and spiritual implications of its content.

Men and women write and read literature for many reasons: to celebrate the beauty of the world as created by God and the beauty of the worlds that humans can imagine through the creative use of language; to protest the presence of evil and injustice in the world, and in so doing, to prompt ourselves and others to meaningful action; to discover, through the metaphors we use and stories we enact, where we have been, who we are, and where we ought to be going; and finally, to see, through a glass darkly, the glory of the Kingdom in which we will sit down at the marriage feast of the Lamb.

APPENDIX

Some Suggestions For Reading Third-World and Minority Literature

Achebe, Chinua. *Things Fall Apart.* 1958 (Nigeria)

Allende, Isabel. *The House of the Spirits.* 1982. (Chile)

Brooks, Gwendolyn. *The Bean Eaters.* 1960. (United States)

Brutus, Dennis. *Letters to Martha and Other Poems fram A South African Prison.* 1968. (South Africa)

Coetzee, J.M. *Waiting for the Barbarians.* 1980. (South Africa)

Douglass, Frederick. *Narrative of the Life of Frederick Douglass, an American Slave.* 1945. (United States)

Endo, Shusako. *Silence.* 1969. (Japan)

Garcia Marquez, Gabriel. *One Hundred Years of Solitude.* 1970. (Colombia)

Gordimer, Nadine. *July's People.* 1981. (South Africa)

Hurston, Zora Neale. *Their Eyes Were Watching God.* 1937. (United States)

La Guma, Alex. *A Walk in the Night and Other Stories.* 1969. (South Africa)

Lao, She. *Crescent Moon and Other Stories.* 1985. (China)

Lu, Yun. *Wandering.* 1981. (China)

Mahfouz, Naguib. "The Conjurer Made Off With the Dish." In *Egyptian Short Stories.* 1978. (Egypt)

Momaday, N. Scott. *House Made of Dawn.* 1969. (United States)

Morrison, Toni. *Beloved.* 1987. (United States)

Naipaul, V.S. *A House for Mr. Biswas.* 1983. (Trinidad)

Narayan, R.K. *Malgudi Days.* 1972. (India)

Selected Short Stories from Pakistan. Ed. Ahmed Ali. 1988. (Pakistan)

Soyinka, Wole. *The Swamp Dwellers.* 1958. (Nigeria)

Yu, Dafu. *Nights of Spring Fever and Other Writings.* 1984. (China)

WORKS CITED

Note: Throughout the book there are numerous citations from works of American and English literature. Unless otherwise noted, the references are to the texts as they are contained in the two anthologies published by W.W. Norton: *The Norton Anthology of American Literature,* ed. Nina Baym et al., and *The Norton Anthology of English Literature,* ed. M. H. Abrams et al. The references to classics from the Western tradition are from *Literature of the Western World,* vol. 1, Wilkie and Hurt, eds., unless otherwise noted.

Unless otherwise indicated, all scriptural references are taken from the *New International Version.*

Abrams, M. H. "Kant and the Theology of Art." *Notre Dame English Journal* 13 (1981): 74–91.
———. *The Mirror and The Lamp: Romantic Theory and the Critical Tradition.* London: Oxford University Press, 1953.
———. *Natural Supernaturalism: Tradition and Revolution in Romantic Literature.* New York: W. W. Norton, 1973.
———. et al., eds. *The Norton Anthology of English Literature.* 5th ed. 2 vols. New York: W. W. Norton, 1986.
Ahlstrom, Sydney. *A Religious History of the American People.* 2 vols. Garden City, NY: Image, 1975.
Alter, Robert and Frank Kermode, eds. *The Literary Guide to the Bible.* Cambridge: Harvard University Press, 1987.
Aristotle. *The Basic Works of Aristotle.* Ed. Richard McKeon. New York: Random House, 1941.
Auden, W. H. *The Dyer's Hand and Other Essays.* New York: Vintage, 1968.
Augustine. *The Confessions of St. Augustine.* Trans. Rex Warner. New York: New American Library, 1963.

————. *On Christian Doctrine*. Trans. D. W. Robertson. Indianapolis: Bobbs-Merrill, 1958.

Bakhtin, M. M. *The Dialogic Imagination*. Trans. Caryl Emerson and Michael Holquist. Austin: University of Texas Press, 1981.

Barfield, Owen. "The Meaning of the Word 'Literal.'" *Metaphor and Symbol*. Eds. L. C. Knights and Basil Cottle. London: Butterworths Scientific Publications, 1960.

Barker, Nicholas P. "A Christian Position on Aesthetic Life and The Fine Arts: II. Human Art Works." Unpublished essay, 1978.

Barthes, Roland. *The Pleasure of the Text*. Trans. Richard Miller. New York: Hill and Wang, 1975.

Baym, Nina, et al. eds. *The Norton Anthology of American Literature*. 2nd ed. 2 vols. New York: Norton, 1985.

Bellah, Robert, et al. *Habits of the Heart: Individualism and Commitment in American Life*. Berkeley: University of California Press, 1985.

Bennett, William J. *To Reclaim a Legacy: A Report on the Humanities in Higher Education*. n.p.: The National Endowment for the Humanities, 1984.

Berry, Wendell. *Home Economics*. San Francisco: North Point Press, 1987.

Bishop, Jim. *The Day Christ Died*. New York: Harper, 1957.

Black, Max. "More About Metaphor." *Metaphor and Thought*. Ed. Andrew Ortony. Cambridge: Cambridge University Press, 1979.

Booth, Wayne C. "Freedom of Interpretation: Bakhtin and the Challenge of Feminist Criticism." *Critical Inquiry* 9 (1982): 45–76.

Calvin, John. *Institutes of The Christian Religion*. Trans. Henry Beveridge. 2 vols. Grand Rapids: Wm. B. Eerdmans, 1953.

Clark, Katerina, and Michael Holquist. *Mikhail Bakhtin*. Cambridge: Harvard University Press, 1984.

Coover, Robert. *The Universal Baseball Association Inc., J. Henry Waugh, Prop*. New York: New American Library, n.d.

Davie, Donald, ed. *The New Oxford Book of Christian Verse*. Oxford: Oxford University Press, 1981.

Dickinson, Emily. "Some keep the Sabbath going to Church." *Final Harvest: Emily Dickinson's Poems*. Ed. Thomas H. Johnson. Boston: Little, Brown, 1961.

Dinesen, Isak. *Seven Gothic Tales*. New York: Vintage Books, 1972.

Donoghue, Denis. *Ferocious Alphabets*. Boston: Little, Brown, 1981.

Eagleton, Terry. *Literary Theory: An Introduction*. Minneapolis: University of Minnesota Press, 1983.

Eliot, T. S. "Religion and Literature." *Religion and Modern Literature: Essays in Theory and Criticism*. Eds. G. B. Tennyson and Edward E. Ericson, Jr. Grand Rapids: Wm. B. Eerdmans, 1975. 21–30.

Emerson, Ralph Waldo. *Essays and Lectures.* New York: The Library of America, 1983.

Federman, Raymond, ed. *Surfiction: Fiction Now . . . And Tomorrow.* Chicago: Swallow, 1975.

Fugard, Athol. *"Master Harold" and the Boys.* New York: Penguin, 1982.

Fowler, Alastair. *Kinds of Literature: An Introduction to the Theory of Genres and Modes.* Cambridge: Harvard University Press, 1982.

Franklin, H. Bruce. "English as an Institution: The Role of Class." *English Literature: Opening up the Canon.* Selected Papers from the English Institute, 1979, New Series 4. Eds. Leslie A. Fiedler and Houston A. Baker, Jr. Baltimore: Johns Hopkins University Press, 1981. 92–106.

Frye, Northrop. *Anatomy of Criticism.* Princeton: Princeton University Press, 1957.

———. *The Educated Imagination.* Bloomington: Indiana University Press, 1964.

Fuller, Edmund. "A Critic's Notes." *The Wall Street Journal,* 5 May 1987: 34.

Gadamer, Hans-Georg. *Truth and Method.* Translation edited by Garrett Barden and John Cumming. New York: Continuum, 1975.

Gass, William H. *Fiction and the Figures of Life.* New York: Alfred Knopf, 1970.

———. "Goodness Knows Nothing of Beauty." *Harper's*, April 1987: 37–44.

Goodfield, June. "Humanity in Science: A Perspective and a Plea." *The Key Reporter* 57 (1977): 2–4.

Grant, Robert M. *A Short History of the Interpretation of the Bible.* New York: Macmillan, 1963.

Hatch, Nathan O., and Mark A. Noll, eds. *The Bible in America.* New York: Oxford University Press, 1982.

Heidegger, Martin. *Being and Time.* Trans. John Macquarrie & Edward Robinson. New York: Harper & Row, 1962.

Heller, Joseph. *Catch-22.* New York: Dell, 1985.

Herbert, George. "Sunday." *The Works of George Herbert.* Ed. F. E. Hutchinson. Oxford: Clarendon Press, 1941.

Holzel, Tom, and Audrey Salkeld. *First on Everest.* New York: Holt, Rinehart & Winston, 1987.

Jung, Carl Gustav. *The Spirit in Man, Art and Literature.* Trans. R.F.C. Hull. London: Routledge & Kegan Paul, 1966. Vol. 15 of *Collected Works of C. G. Jung.* 20 vols. 1953–1979.

Kant, Immanuel. *Critique of Judgment.* Trans. James C. Meredith. *The*

Philosophy of Kant. Ed. Carl J. Friedrich. New York: Modern Library, 1949.

Kermode, Frank. *The Sense of an Ending: Studies in the Theory of Fiction.* New York: Oxford University Press, 1967.

Knight, George Wilson. *The Wheel of Fire.* London: Methuen, 1949.

La Guma, Alex. *A Walk in the Night and Other Stories.* Evanston: Northwestern University Press, 1967.

Langbaum, Robert. *Isak Dinesen's Art: The Gayety of Vision.* Chicago: University of Chicago Press, 1975.

Langer, Suzanne. "The Comic Rhythm." *Feeling and Form: A Theory of Art.* New York: Charles Scribner's Sons, 1953. 326–350.

Lentricchia, Frank. *After the New Criticism.* Chicago: University of Chicago Press, 1980.

Lewis, C. S. *The Chronicles of Narnia.* 7 volumes. New York: Macmillan, 1970.

———. *The Four Loves.* New York: Harcourt Brace Jovanovich, 1960.

———. *The Pilgrim's Regress.* Grand Rapids: Wm. B. Eerdmans, 1958.

———. *Till We Have Faces: A Myth Retold.* New York: Harcourt Brace, 1956.

———. *The Weight of Glory and Other Addresses.* New York: Macmillan, 1980.

Löwith, Karl. *Meaning in History.* Chicago: University of Chicago Press, 1949.

Lowell, Robert. "King David Old." *History.* New York: Farrar, Straus & Giroux, 1973.

Lundin, Roger, Anthony C. Thiselton, and Clarence Walhout. *The Responsibility of Hermeneutics.* Grand Rapids: Wm. B. Eerdmans, 1985.

McFarland, Thomas. *Originality and Imagination.* Baltimore: Johns Hopkins University Press, 1985.

MacIntyre, Alasdair. *After Virtue: A Study in Moral Theory.* 2nd ed. Notre Dame: University of Notre Dame Press, 1984.

Marsden, George M. "A Christian Perspective for the Teaching of History." *A Christian View of History?* Eds. George Marsden and Frank Roberts. Grand Rapids: Wm. B. Eerdmans, 1975.

MacLeish, Archibald. *J.B.* Boston: Houghton, Mifflin, 1958.

May, Henry F. *The Enlightenment in America.* Oxford: Oxford University Press, 1976.

Melville, Herman. *Moby-Dick.* Eds. Harrison Hayford and Hershel Parker. New York: Norton, 1967.

Morris, Adalaide. "Dick, Jane, and American Literature: Fighting with Canons." *College English* 47 (1985): 467–481.

Nims, John Frederick. *Western Wind: An Introduction to Poetry.* 2nd ed. New York: Random House, 1983.

O'Connor, Flannery, "Catholic Novelists and Their Readers." *Mystery and Manners.* Eds. Sally and Robert Fitzgerald. New York: Farrar, Straus & Giroux, 1961. 169–190.

Paton, Alan. *Cry, the Beloved Country.* New York: Scribners, 1948.

Pelikan, Jaroslav. *The Christian Tradition: A History of the Development of Doctrine. Vol I: The Emergence of the Catholic Tradition (100–600).* Chicago: University of Chicago Press, 1971.

———. *The Christian Tradition: A History of the Development of Doctrine. Vol 4: Reformation of Church and Dogma (1300–1700).* Chicago: University of Chicago Press, 1984.

Ricoeur, Paul. *The Conflict of Interpretations.* Ed. Don Ihde. Evanston: Northwestern University Press, 1974.

———. *Hermeneutics and the Human Sciences.* Trans. and ed. John B. Thompson. Cambridge: Cambridge University Press, 1981.

———. "The Metaphorical Process as Cognition, Imagination, and Feeling." *On Metaphor.* Ed. Sheldon Sacks. Chicago: University of Chicago Press, 1979. 141–157.

———. *The Rule of Metaphor: Multi-disciplinary Studies of the Creation of Meaning in Language.* Trans. Robert Czerny with Kathleen McLaughlin and John Costello, SJ. Toronto: University of Toronto Press, 1977.

———. *The Symbolism of Evil.* Trans. Emerson Buchanan. Boston: Beacon Press, 1967.

Ryken, Leland. *The Literature of the Bible.* Grand Rapids: Zondervan, 1974.

Scholes, Robert. *Textual Power: Literary Theory and the Teaching of English.* New Haven: Yale University Press, 1985.

Schultze, Quentin. *Television: Manna from Hollywood.* Grand Rapids: Zondervan, 1986.

Scott, Nathan A., Jr. "The Bias of Comedy and the Narrow Escape into Faith." *The Christian Scholar* 44 (1961): 9–39.

Seerveld, Calvin. *Rainbows for the Fallen World: Aesthetic Life and Artistic Task.* Downsview, Ontario: Toronto Tuppence Press, 1980.

Shakespeare, William. *A Midsummer Night's Dream. The Complete Pelican Shakespeare.* Ed. Alfred Harbage. New York: Viking, 1969.

———. *The Merry Wives of Windsor. The Complete Pelican Shakespeare.* Ed. Alfred Harbage. New York: Viking, 1969.

Showalter, Elaine. "The Feminist Critical Revolution." *The New Feminist Criticism: Essays on Women, Literature, and Theory.* Ed. Elaine Showalter. New York: Pantheon, 1985. 3–17.

Spengemann, William. *The Adventurous Muse: The Poetics of American Fiction, 1789–1900.* New Haven: Yale University Press, 1977.

Steiner, George. *In Bluebeard's Castle: Some Notes Towards the Redefinition of Culture.* London: Yale University Press, 1971.

Stoppard, Tom. *Rosencrantz and Gildenstern Are Dead.* New York: Grove Press, 1967.

Thielicke, Helmut. *The Evangelical Faith, Vol. 1: Prolegomena: The Relation of Theology to Modern Thought-Forms.* Trans. and ed. Geoffrey W. Bromiley. Grand Rapids: Wm. B. Eerdmans, 1974.

Timmerman, John H. "Typology and Biblical Consistency in *Billy Budd.*" *Notre Dame English Journal* 15 (1983): 23–28.

Todorov, Tzvetan. *Theories of the Symbol.* Trans. Catherine Porter. Ithaca: Cornell University Press, 1982.

Tompkins, Jane. *Sensational Designs: The Cultural Work of American Fiction 1790–1860.* New York: Oxford University Press, 1985.

Vos, Nelvin. *The Drama of Comedy: Victim and Victor.* Richmond: John Knox, 1966.

Weinsheimer, Joel C. *Gadamer's Hermeneutics: A Reading of* Truth and Method. New Haven: Yale University Press, 1985.

Weisbuch, Robert. *Atlantic Double-Cross: American Literature and British Influence in the Age of Emerson.* Chicago: University of Chicago Press, 1986.

Wiesel, Elie. *Night.* Trans. Stella Rodway. New York: Avon, 1960.

Wilkie, Brian, and James Hurt, eds. *Literature of the Western World.* Vol. 1. New York: Macmillan, 1984.

Williams, Tennessee. *The Glass Menagerie. The Health Guide to Literature.* Eds. David Bergman and Daniel Mark Epstein. Lexington, MA: D.C. Heath, 1984. 968–1010.

Wolterstorff, Nicholas. *Art in Action: Toward a Christian Aesthetic.* Grand Rapids: Wm. B. Eerdmans, 1980.

Woodward, Kenneth L. "Inspirational Romances." *Newsweek,* 20 February 1984: 69.

Woolf, Virginia. *A Room of One's Own.* New York: Harcourt Brace Jovanovich, 1957.

Zylstra, Henry. *Testament of Vision.* Grand Rapids: Wm. B. Eerdmans, 1958.

GENERAL INDEX

SCRIPTURE REFERENCES